# Social, Political, and Economic Issues in Black America

## Volume IV

William Monroe Trotter Institute
University of Massachusetts at Boston

1990

© 1990 by William Monroe Trotter Institute
ISBN 1-878358-03-0

# Table of Contents

Preface ................................................................. v

1. Stratification and Subordination:
   Change and Continuity
       E. Yvonne Moss and Wornie L. Reed ................. 1

2. Race and Inequality in the Managerial Age
       William Darity, Jr. ..................................... 29

3. Black Political Participation:
   The Search for Power
       E. Yvonne Moss ........................................ 83

4. The Search for Voice:
   Ideology and Perspective in the Black Community
       Phillip L. Clay ......................................... 119

Appendix: Assessment of the Status of African-Americans
Project Study Group Members and Contributors ............ 147

# Preface

In the Spring of 1987 the William Monroe Trotter Institute at the University of Massachusetts at Boston initiated a project entitled, "The Assessment of the Status of African-Americans." Thirty-five scholars were organized into study groups, one for each of six topics: education; employment, income, and occupations; political participation and the administration of justice; social and cultural change; health status and medical care; and the family. The study groups were established to analyze the status of African-Americans in each of the topical areas in anticipation of the results and analyses of the National Research Council's Study Committee on the Status of Black Americans. We wanted to have the widest possible discussion of the present condition of blacks and the social policy implications of that condition.

The multidisciplinary group of scholars comprising the study groups included persons from all sections of the country and from varied settings–private and public universities, historically black universities, and private agencies. A list of these scholars by study group is given in the Appendix. Each of the study groups met and drafted an agenda for examining significant issues under their respective topics. Members chose issues from this agenda within their areas of expertise and identified other scholars who had written extensively on other issues on the agenda. These other scholars made a variety of contributions, including original papers, reprints, notes and materials, and/or substantial commentaries on draft documents.

Despite the pressures of limited time and limited financial support for this work, six volumes were produced:

Volume I: *Summary*
Volume II: *Research on the African-American Family: A Holistic Perspective*
Volume III: *Education of African-Americans*
Volume IV: *Social, Political, and Economic Issues in Black America*
Volume V: *Health and Medical Care of African-Americans*
Volume VI: *Critiques of the NRC Study,* A Common Destiny: Blacks and American Society

Each of the study groups developed its own conclusions and policy recommendations. The individual authors in these volumes used papers and materials generated by the members of their respective study groups in preparing their articles.

In addition to study group members and other contributors, we are indebted to a number of individuals for the production of this study. We owe thanks to Phillip Hallen and the Maurice Falk Foundation for underwriting the costs of producing these volumes. Special thanks are also offered to the following persons: our editors–Duncan Nelson, Manuscript Editor; Linda Kluz and Suzanne Baker, Production Editors; the office staff–Eva Hendricks, Gemima Remy and Tina Wilson; and Assistant Director Frances Stubbs.

Wornie L. Reed

# 1
# Stratification and Subordination: Change and Continuity

E. Yvonne Moss and Wornie L. Reed

One of the measures used to gauge progress made by African-Americans in gaining equal opportunity has been to compare and contrast the status of black Americans to that of white Americans using various social indices. Historically, the status of blacks relative to whites has been one of subordination; race has been a primary factor in determining social stratification and political status. Relations between white and black Americans were established during slavery and the Jim Crow era of segregation. In the infamous *Dred Scott* decision, U.S. Supreme Court Chief Justice Taney articulated the fundamental nature of this system of racial stratification: "Blacks have no rights which whites are bound to respect" (Bell, 1980a).

James Baldwin perceptively observed that in the sea change from the old worlds to the new, French, English, Spanish, and other Europeans "became white," while the Tokolor, Mandinka, Fulani, and other Africans "became black" (Baldwin, 1985). Black and white became racial labels denoting power and status. Blacks were slaves; whites were free. Elimination of property requirements in the nineteenth century extended the franchise to all white men, and the passage of the Nineteenth Amendment (in the twentieth century) extended the franchise to white women. Not until the passage of the Voting Rights Act of 1965 was the franchise extended to all black Americans; and not until the *Brown* decision of 1954 were black Americans granted equal protection under the law. The Civil War outlawed slavery, but it did not eliminate stratification and privilege based on race. White domination continued through segregation laws and practices. The *Brown* decision, the civil rights movement, the Civil Rights Act of 1964, and the Voting Rights Act of 1965 ushered in a new era of race relations. After 300 years of slavery and 100 years of legalized racial oppression, the relations between white and black Americans were now to be based on "equality." The "age of equality," however, has not been accompanied by an end to white domination.

Scholars in this study have sought to evaluate developments in race relations, particularly since 1940, by examining racial stratification, subordination, and change in various areas of American life. Our general conclusion is that despite improvements in various aspects of American life, racial stratification has not changed in any fundamental sense. In addition to the structural mechanisms that perpetuate differential status researchers point to social factors–attitudes, values, ideology, and racial violence–that reinforce racial domination. Legal doctrines and the courts have always provided justification and legality for whatever structural form the system of racial stratification has taken. Historically, the U.S. Constitution has been one of the primary supports for white supremacy.

## From Slavery to Equality

Relations between black and white Americans are now established by the equality expectations based on the Constitution. This document, which originally sanctioned slavery, then segregation, has since 1954 given legal sanction to the principle of equality. At the time of the American Revolution slavery was sanctioned by the Constitution as a form of white property rights. The concepts of equality articulated by colonists in revolt blurred class distinctions between poor and rich whites, promoting affinity and solidarity at a time when these class distinctions could have undermined the war of liberation against the British.

After independence, an expansion of civil liberties for whites was accompanied by a contraction of civil rights for blacks. Slavery, recognized in the Constitution as a political and economic phenomenon rather than a moral one, provided the essential ingredient by which lower-class whites and upper-class whites could share a common identity as "free men." Slavery, and the racism that justified it, provided a way by which poor whites could simultaneously feel superior to enslaved blacks and equal to rich whites in spite of a distinctly different social and class status. In order to maintain this white American kinship, there was the need to keep black Americans in "their place." Citizenship, national identity, and social status in the emerging United States were increasingly defined in terms of race and color. Although Jacksonian Democracy removed property qualifications to extend the franchise for white males, in 1840 most free blacks were legally denied the right to vote.

From the beginning, the Constitution gave the wealthy "planter class" (approximately 7% of all slaveholders) disproportionate power, both nationally and locally. A majority of the justices on the Supreme Court between 1789 and 1865 were themselves slaveowners. Up until the Civil War, constitutional interpretation did not violate the economic and political imperatives of a slave economy dominated by a white, male, landed aristocracy.

After the war, the Civil War Amendments (Thirteenth, Fourteenth, and Fifteenth) along with Reconstruction provided a halting start toward a new basis of race relations. These nascent efforts were brought to an end, however, with the Hayes-Tilden Compromise in 1877 and the withdrawal of Union troops from the South. Racial discrimination against blacks increased at the same time that political democratization increased for whites. In a major test of the Fourteenth Amendment, the Supreme Court legitimized corporations but not the rights of black citizens in the 1873 *Slaughter-House Case(s)*. In those cases, the due process clause of the Fourteenth Amendment, which would become so vital to the restructuring of black/white relations in the mid-twentieth century, was interpreted to provide more protection for corporations (deemed legally to be "persons") than to African-Americans (Bell, 1980b).

The struggles of black Americans and their allies against segregation during the nineteenth and twentieth centuries culminated in the *Brown* decisions (1954 and 1955), the Civil Rights Act of 1964, and the Voting Rights Act of 1965. The White House's support for the modern civil rights movement of the sixties seemed to herald at long last the arrival of the equality revolution. For the first time since the existence of the Freedmen's Bureau during the Reconstruction period, governments not only made laws but constituted themselves as instruments of egalitarian policy. Above all, the courts were now obliged to examine constitutional principles in the light of egalitarian pressures.

With the emergence of the "age of equality," a number of important questions have been raised about race relations, law, and stratification. Can equality expectations eliminate racism and stratification by race and assure that there are no special advantages distributed according to race? Are there economic incentives and penalties capable of inducing the white elite to forsake segregation? And, is it possible that equality will actually sustain, rather than relieve, white domination?

Examination of the issues raised by such questions has led some scholars to argue that although the application of equality is perceived as the extension of democratic principles to all–regardless of race, creed, color, or sex–it is more likely that the equality principle is serving white interests more than those of black people. Historically, advances for African-Americans have been the result of policies primarily intended to serve white interests rather than to provide remedies for racial injustices (Bell, 1980b). Thus, scholars need to examine the contemporary "age of equality" for mechanisms that promote white self-interests at the expense of African-Americans.

For instance, one social analyst concludes that just as segregation "shifted" racism out of slavery to assure white exploitation of black labor, so equality "shifts" racism out of segregation to assure the economic demise rather than the exploitation of black people. Socioeconomic disparities coexist with the opportunity for equal rights under the Constitution. Supreme Court rulings have not outlawed racism, it is argued, but instead have actually endorsed a new form of racism to justify white oppression of black Americans. The notion of equality today, then, is as much a racist doctrine as were slavery and segregation (Wilhelm, 1987).

The established image of "equality" has meant that African-Americans can possess all manner of civil rights in the abstract, but little property. Wealth remains in white hands so that even under this so-called "equality" the social results are the same. The equality doctrine both masks and justifies the prevailing inequalities. Mechanisms other than color distinction are employed to subjugate black citizens. Growing disparities between black and white Americans coincide with the legal expansion of equal rights. The vigorous replacement of segregation by equality occurs at the same time that black people are being eliminated from the economy.

## Socioeconomic Status

Economically, black America is in crisis. The annual income of black families is 57% of white families. The net worth of black American families in 1986 was $3,397, compared to $39,135 for whites families, a difference of almost 1200%. In 1985 a National Urban League study indicated that with persistent unemployment and expanding poverty, African-Americans were being left out of the nation's economic recovery. If current trends continue to the year 2000, only 30% of all black men will be employed. Just as the abolition of slavery did not eradicate racism nor the patterns of structural bias based on race, the equality doctrine has also failed to do so. Ironically, contemporary interpretations of the equality principle based on the Constitution seek a "color-blind" society that perpetuates inequality based on race.

When economics, employment, and social class are examined the continued importance of race is clearly evident. While discrimination has lessened in jobs and training programs, racially exclusive practices remain. Limitations on mobility because of race affect the black elite as well as the black poor. The most strikingly favorable indication of racial change is the growth of the middle class among African-Americans. In 1982, using constant dollars, almost 25% of black families had incomes over $25,000 as compared to 8.7% in 1960 (Taylor, 1984).

This occupational mobility is a product of three factors: affirmative action, the expansion of public sector employment, and higher levels of education. Between 1966 and 1982 the number of black college students increased from 340,000 to over one million. A number of indicators, however, tend to suggest that such mobility may be slowed if not reversed in the near future. Between 1980 and 1984, black college enrollment dropped by 3%. Concomitantly, the more precarious economic status of black members of the middle class makes them more vulnerable than their white counterparts to economic downturns, government budget cuts, and changes in affirmative action policy.

The black middle class is proportionately smaller than the white middle class and is skewed more toward the lower than the upper part of the statistical group. Black professionals occupy lower paying jobs in lower prestige fields than white professionals. Black families tend to be more dependent on two or more wage-earners to maintain their middle-class status than are white families. Higher proportions of married women in black households work than married women in white households. These factors along with a lower net worth and fewer resources means that black middle-class families are not as able as white middle-class families to transmit their class position to their children. In some cities–Atlanta, Philadelphia, New York, Los Angeles, Chicago, Oakland, and the District of Columbia, for example–the growth of middle-class economic status is still significant. However, there is less hope generally for economic advancement for other African-Americans trapped in poverty in urban and rural areas than there was in the sixties.

Noteworthy progress was made between 1959 and 1969 in reducing poverty among African-Americans. The percentage of black citizens who were poor dropped in that decade from 45% to 25%, and the official black family poverty rate declined from 48% to 28%. The net reduction in the number of poor black families was 494,000. However, during the 1970s this black economic progress was reversed as the percentage of blacks who were poor in 1979 had declined less than .5% during that decade, from 28% to 27.6%, and the black portion of the poor increased to 31%. Over 300,000 more black families were poor in 1979 than in 1969, thus canceling the gains made in the previous decade (Cross, 1984).

The dimensions of the socioeconomic crisis are even more evident from an examination of the consequences of these worsening economic conditions. More than one-half of all black children grow up in poverty. Unemployment among black teenagers has increased. Many young black men, unsuccessful in school and unable to find legitimate work, turn to hustling and crime. Homicide has become a leading cause of death among young black females as well as among young black males. The economic crisis among the poor has reduced the proportion of black men who work. Traditionally, blacks have been more likely than white men to be in the labor force. Since 1970, however, blacks have been less likely to be in the labor force (Swinton, 1990) and many of these workers are unemployed or underemployed. Some analysts estimate that less than one-half of black men are engaged in steady work.

## Residential Segregation

In the area of housing, racial bias has remained pervasive. Throughout most of the half century that the federal government has been involved in housing and urban development, national policies have compounded and supported the discriminatory practices of realtors, banks, insurance companies, and lending companies. A review of major national policy initiatives by officials in the legislative, executive, and judicial branches of government indicates that during most of the past 50 years federal policies favored segregation and discrimination in housing.

Housing discrimination and the urbanization of blacks throughout the country have led to what some call the development of black "ghettos." Kenneth Clark, for example, referring to this phenomenon, has written: "The dark ghetto's invisible walls have been created by the white society, by those who have power, both to confine those who have *no* power and to perpetuate their powerlessness." He continues, "The dark ghettos are social, political, educational, and–above all–economic colonies. Their inhabitants are subject peoples, victims of the greed, cruelty, insensitivity, guilt, and fear of their masters" (Clark, 1965, p. 11).

In the same vein, the National Advisory Commission on Civil Disorders, established after the widespread destruction accompanying rebellions in black communities throughout the United States, reported in 1968 that "What white Americans have never understood–but what the Negro can never forget–is that white society is deeply implicated in the ghetto. White institutions created it, white institutions maintain it, and white society condones it" (U.S. National Advisory Commission on Civil Disorders, 1968, p. 2).

The federal government has been involved in housing and urban development for nearly half a century, and throughout most of that time the policies of the government favored segregation and discrimination against minorities in housing. It was not until 1962 that minimal steps were taken to curb these practices. This has led to the conclusion that "Indeed, the net effect of Federal involvement in housing and urban development has been largely to perpetuate housing discrimination and patterns of housing segregation. In many cases, the Federal government has been a major force in exacerbating those problems" (U.S. Commission on Civil Rights, 1983, p. 133).

The following represent the major legislative, executive, and judicial actions supporting fair housing policies since 1940:

- 1948: In *Shelley v. Kraemer* (1948) the Supreme Court held that judicial enforcement of racially restrictive covenants violated the Fourteenth Amendment to the Constitution.

- 1962: President John Kennedy issued Executive Order 11063 on equal opportunity in housing. The order was designed to eliminate discrimination in federally assisted housing.

- 1964: Title VI of the Civil Rights Act was enacted, prohibiting programs or activities receiving federal assistance by way of loan or grant.

- 1968: Congress passed the Civil Rights Act of 1968. This law established the "policy of the United States to provide, within Constitutional limitations, for fair housing throughout the United States." This Act contains Title VIII, which prohibits discrimination in most of the nation's housing, both public and private. It also prohibits discrimination in mortgage lending and the advertising of housing. There have also been amendments to strengthen the law in the years since its first enactment.

- 1968: In *Jones v. Mayer* (1968) the Supreme Court upheld a 1866 civil rights law that bars "all racial discrimination, private and public, in the sale or rental of property."

- 1968: The Housing and Urban Development Act of 1968 was enacted establishing new programs of subsidized housing for lower income families.

Prior to 1962 there were three separate housing markets in the United States: one for blacks, one for whites, and one for mixed occupancy (U.S. Commission on Civil Rights, 1983, p. 3). The federal government accepted and even supported these discriminatory practices. Racial homogeneity was considered to be essential for stability in rental areas, and it was felt that any change in occupancy patterns would lead to a decline in property values. At the same time blacks were excluded from the suburbs. The Executive Order of the President in 1962 did little, if anything, to foster fair housing policies.

The 1964 Civil Rights Act likewise had little or no effect on open housing. However, four year later the Civil Rights Act of 1968 established for the first time a comprehensive fair housing program, making it illegal to discriminate in almost all housing, public and private. What was lacking, however, was vigorous enforcement of the provisions of this Act.

Little has been accomplished toward the goal of fair housing, and since the beginning of the Reagan administration in 1981 the federal government has moved away from vigorously enforcing fair housing laws, maintaining that voluntary compliance was the principal mechanism for fair housing (U.S. Commission on Civil Rights, 1983, pp. 140-141). This hardly serves the cause of fair housing, for voluntary compliance means no compliance. Among the first acts of this administration was the withdrawal of the interpretative regulations of the Civil Rights Act of 1968. The Department of Justice has curtailed its enforcement efforts to the point where it has virtually abandoned the area of fair housing. And, the government has reduced, and in some cases eliminated, efforts to eliminate the data required to determine whether violations of the Civil Rights of 1968 had taken place. In short, one is forced to agree with the following assessment:

> The federal government currently exhibits no enthusiasm in carrying out its statutory and constitutional mandates of nondiscrimination in housing. Indeed, the government, measured by its action during the present administration, appears to be engaged in an effort to dismantle the very legal and programmatic structure by which the fragile foundation of fair housing has been painfully built over the past three decades. (U.S. Commission on Civil Rights, 1983, p. 134)

Discrimination in housing today remains pervasive, as several studies indicate (Danielson, 1976; Feagin and Feagin, 1986; National Committee Against Discrimination in Housing (n.d.); Struyk, 1976; U.S. Commission on Civil Rights, 1974; U.S. Commission on Civil Rights, 1975; U.S. Department of Housing and Urban Development, 1984). Discrimination is widespread in the rental and sales of housing, in urban and suburban regions, and in public and private housing. Although the federal government finally has a stated policy of fair housing for all Americans, it has been far from diligent in curbing housing discrimination. The Department of Housing and Urban Development and the Department of Justice are responsible for compliance with fair housing laws, but neither agency has effectively enforced the laws.

The Housing Market Practices Survey (U.S. Department of Housing and Urban Development, 1979), for example, conducted one of the largest studies of its type in 1977 and concluded that:

- Discrimination in the housing market persists on a significant scale in all areas of the United States.

- The practices are frequently subtle and require sophisticated techniques for detection.

- Massive skillful enforcement efforts will be required to eradicate these practices.

The residential segregation of blacks actually increased in the 1940s, 1950s, and 1960s. Between 1950 and 1970 black neighborhoods in 20 large cities, where they represented three-fourths of the population, increased from 30% to 51% while the proportion of blacks in mixed neighborhoods with 25% or fewer blacks declined from 25% to 16% (Levitan et al. 1973, p. 227).

One of the few empirical measures of discrimination in housing is the segregation index. Developed by Karl E. Taeuber and Alma F. Taeuber, the index can be used to measure increases in housing segregation over time and to compare cities and regions of the country. It assumes values between 0 and 100. The higher the index, the greater the degree of racial segregation; conversely, the lower the index, the less the degree of racial segregation in housing. For example, the Taeubers report that Indianapolis, Indiana, had a segregation index of 90.4 in 1940, 91.4 in 1950, and 91.6 in 1960. This means that in Indianapolis the extent of segregation in housing increased steadily for three decades (Taeuber and Taeuber, 1972, p. 40).

As the Taeubers report, "In a city where Negroes constitute half of the population, the residents of any city block would be about equally divided between Negroes and whites. In a city where Negroes constitute 10 percent of the population, one of every ten households in each block might be expected to be Negro" (p. 29). The index has been computed for several decades, although the number of cities included in each period varies.

Taeuber and Taeuber's national housing segregation index indicates that America's cities are only slightly less segregated today than they were in 1940. The index in 1940 was 85.2. By 1950 that figure had worsened to 87.3. In 1960 there was a slight drop to 86.1, but the segregation index increased during that decade to 87.0. The decade from 1970 to 1980 showed a drop from 87.0 to 81.0. Clearly, America's neighborhoods continue to be "homogeneous" (racially segregated) despite new laws and public proclamations (Reed, 1989).

As these data indicate, discrimination in housing is widespread, and there appears to be little promise for substantially reducing it in the near future. One writer has suggested that with the 6-point drop in the average segregation index for urban areas in the decade of the 1970s, "It will take another half century to half desegregate these cities. Some cities, such as Chicago, St. Louis, and Washington, will take centuries to be fully desegregated" (U.S. Commission on Civil Rights, 1983, p. 144).

Extensive suburbanization occurred in the United States after World War II, but suburban housing was intended for whites, not blacks. Although it is estimated that the number of blacks living in the suburbs increased by 28.3%, from 758,000 to 3,433,000 between 1960 and 1970, such growth was not uniform throughout the country (U.S. Commission on Civil Rights, 1983, p. 31). For example, it is estimated that one-sixth of the increase was in the suburbs of Washington, DC. In addition, seven standard metropolitan statistical areas contained about 55% of black suburbanites in 1980 (U.S. Commission on Civil Rights, 1983, p. 31).

From 1950 through 1970, blacks accounted for slightly more than 5% of suburban residents (Dolce, 1976, p. 82). During the decade of the 1970s the metropolitan areas with the largest volumes of black suburban growth experienced low or declining rates of growth. Data indicate that the black population of the suburbs rose from 2.5 million in 1960 to 3.6 million in 1970, and nearly 6.2 million in 1980 (U.S. Commission on Civil Rights, 1983, p. 4). The number of black suburbanites increased because ". . . in a number of cities, ghettos have expanded beyond the city line and into the inner suburbs" (Orfield, 1981, p. 54).

Most suburban blacks live in the rings surrounding the largest cities in the country. It is estimated that the proportion of blacks in these areas was about 3% for decades (Farley, 1970, p. 514). In the 1960s the black population in the suburban rings increased slightly. In addition to the suburban rings, older, more densely populated suburbs witnessed a growth in black population, as did some of the new suburban developments.

The U.S. Commission on Civil Rights reported in 1975 that while suburban blacks are more integrated with whites than those in central cities, most suburban blacks live in places that "resemble their sister central cities rather than new growth, suburban areas and hence do not fit the common concept of suburbs" (U.S. Commission on Civil Rights, 1975, p. 131). By 1970, only one suburban resident in 20 was black, "and even then was likely to reside in a disproportionately black suburb next to a central city ghetto. . . . This overwhelming degree of segregation seems unlikely to have occurred merely by chance" (Feagin and Feagin, 1986, p. 86).

One must conclude that fair housing practices are virtually nonexistent in America's suburbs. Although some blacks have moved to the suburbs, especially since 1960, this in no way indicates a change in residential patterns for African-Americans. They continue to be concentrated in central cities throughout the country, and where they have moved to the suburbs, it has been in those areas adjacent to large cities. Hence, the "residential segregation patterns of central cities are reappearing in the suburbs" (Farley, 1970, p. 527).

The slow desegregation of white suburbs and neighborhoods is only one aspect of the housing crisis. Progress toward access to safe, affordable, adequate housing has been nil. Public housing projects have generally been failures; often these projects have further isolated poor black people from the rest of society. Inadequate delivery of public services and the absence of competitive and diverse private retail and financial services contribute to the general crisis in housing as well as to other aspects of social and economic deprivation.

## White Attitudes

Economic and social deprivation have been the consequences of racial stratification. The system of domination that institutionalizes race-based access to opportunity structures is both reflected in and reinforced by attitudes of white and black Americans. It is interesting to note that the longest running topic in survey research has been the evaluation of white attitudes towards African-Americans. Since World War II, issues related to race in survey research have changed in two ways: the kinds of issues addressed and the ascriptive characteristics associated with the attributes "progressive" and "regressive." Changes in law have made many issues moot. Surveys of white attitudes today indicate that regional differences are less distinct. White attitudes toward black Americans have become more uniform throughout the country.

White Americans still exhibit the duality of orientation that Ellison (1964) labeled "ethical schizophrenia" in the 1940s. By this he meant that white Americans demonstrated a sincere belief in the values of democracy, while condoning and justifying decidedly undemocratic treatment of black citizens. Today scholars use the term "symbolic racism" to explain how white Americans can hold egalitarian general racial attitudes at the same time as they disapprove or oppose policies that seek to operationalize equality. (Cf. Schuman et al. 1985; Bobo, 1983; Kinder and Sears, 1981; McConahay and Hough, 1976).

There have been increases in both interracial attitudes about social contact and (to a lesser extent) increases in black penetration of white neighborhoods and churches. But the data suggest that the increases in the social and spatial *proximity* of blacks and whites do not necessarily result in increased social *interaction* (Smith, 1988).

At face value, whites seem to adhere to the principles of racial equality and interaction. But whenever the contexts of such interaction are specified, opposition is raised. A look at post-World War II changes in attitudes toward varying degrees of school desegregation may shed some light on this issue. As shown in table 1-1, between 1958 and 1986 almost all whites came to accept the presence of a few blacks in school with their children. But note that if the question is posed such that half of the children in the desegregated school are black, tolerance drops an average of approximately 20%. When the question is asked about majority black schools, as many as half of those tolerant of half-black schools become intolerant. Further, while there are increases in tolerance of a few blacks and half-black schools over time, there is relatively little improvement in white attitudes toward majority black schools.

## Table 1-1

Attitudes of Whites Toward Varying Degrees
of School Desegregation, 1958-1986[a]

| Survey Year | Percent in Favor of Attending Schools With | | |
|---|---|---|---|
| | A Few Black Students | 50% Black Students | >50% Black Students |
| 1958[b] | 74.2 | 48.5 | 31.6 |
| 1959 | 79.6 | 52.8 | 29.7 |
| 1963 | 77.8 | 48.4 | 26.7 |
| 1965[c] | 83.2 | 57.9 | 31.7 |
| 1966 | 87.5 | 57.3 | 32.4 |
| 1969 | 88.4 | 61.8 | 34.6 |
| 1970[c] | 91.0 | 68.4 | 35.4 |
| 1972 | 94.0 | 74.7 | 44.8 |
| 1973 | 91.8 | 64.4 | 91.0 |
| 1974 | 95.7 | 66.9 | 33.4 |
| 1975[c] | 94.1 | 68.1 | 36.0 |
| 1977 | 92.8 | 73.5 | 35.8 |
| 1978[c] | 93.8 | 69.0 | 36.3 |
| 1980 | 94.2 | 71.6 | 38.4 |
| 1982 | 95.8 | 79.4 | 45.5 |
| 1983 | 96.5 | 74.9 | 35.1 |
| 1985 | 95.7 | 77.6 | 40.2 |
| 1986 | 96.2 | 76.4 | 36.3 |

[a]Over 96.2% of all nonblack respondents are white. Includes only those respondents living in a home with school-aged children.

[b]All surveys conducted by the American Institute of Public Opinion (Gallup) or the National Opinion Research Center (NORC). All sampling errors $\leq 5\%$.

[c]These issues appeared in two Gallup surveys in both 1965 and 1970 and in one Gallup and one NORC survey in both 1975 and 1978. The percentage above are the mean results from both surveys in those years.

Source: Racial Insularity at the Core: Contemporary American Racial Attitudes, by A. Wade Smith, 1988, *Trotter Review*, 2 (2) p. 11, Boston, MA: University of Massachusetts, William Monroe Trotter Institute.

In schools with a few blacks, the likelihood of any one white child interacting with a black child is extremely low. But, all other things being equal, in half-black schools this likelihood of interracial interaction theoretically increases to around 50%, and in majority black schools it should exceed 50%. So as long as the *intensity* of the interracial experience is quite low, whites seem more willing to participate. But as this intensity increases, the attractiveness of the situation decreases. The racial attitudes of whites are directly proportional to amount of interaction structured by the potential interracial context. Note that the desegregation of public accommodations, transportation, etc., can be accepted because the amount of interaction it *compels* for participants is low, while the relatively intense social contact of interracial dining is avoided.

This group position approach was first postulated by Blumer (1958) and empirically validated in time-series analyses of both attitudes toward interracial housing (Smith, 1982), and school desegregation (Smith, 1981). While the largest component of racial attitude change involves simultaneous change across all subgroups of whites, a substantial component of the incremental *increase in tolerance* over time stems from cohort replacement, i.e., younger persons replacing older persons in the surveys. Further, *decreases in tolerance* among whites accrue as a result of increased educational attainment over time (Smith, 1985).

This data and the results of other surveys suggest that not much racial attitude change should be expected in the near future. All of the big (and easy) changes have been incorporated into public policy. Partially as a result, there is little interest in white attitudes regarding these moot issues. With the possible exception of school desegregation, those areas of racial contact remaining are beyond the regulation of law. In short, the amount of interracial personal contact any white experiences is the result of a series of extremely personal decisions, and it seems as though most will not extend themselves very much in that direction.

It appears that just as whites do not seem to be extending themselves toward blacks, they also do not want blacks to intrude into their lives. Both Gallup and NORC have surveyed whites on their attitudes regarding the intrusion of blacks into "their world." Over time, these four specific questions were repeated most frequently:

Which statement comes closest to how you, yourself, feel: Blacks shouldn't push themselves where they are not wanted. (Agree strongly, agree slightly, disagree slightly, disagree strongly)

White people have a right to keep blacks out of their neighborhoods if they want to, and blacks should respect that right. (Agree strongly, agree slightly, disagree slightly, disagree strongly)

Suppose there is a community-wide vote on the general housing issue. There are two possible laws to vote on (respondent reads an open and a restricted housing law). Which law would you vote for?

In general, do you favor or oppose busing of black and white school children from one district to another?

According to table 1-2, only a little more than a third of all whites would accept the legitimacy of blacks pushing for desegregation in the face of white resistance. In other words, even in the 1980s, a sentiment of racial insularity exists among an overwhelming majority of nonblacks. Note that there has only been a slight erosion in these feelings since the 1960s. It seems that while a majority of the white population willingly coexists with blacks in desegregated work, school, and other public settings, in reality they want as little to do with blacks as possible.

This sentiment becomes glaringly apparent when specific public policies surrounding interracial contact are at issue. While the overwhelming majority would limit such actions, more than a quarter of all whites would give some respect to the "right" of whites to bar blacks from their neighborhoods (see table 1-2), and these respondents would call for blacks to yield a similar respect In other words, a substantial plurality of whites see nothing wrong in restrictive covenants and other limitations to free-market real estate activities that are designed specifically to preserve the racial integrity of a community.

Table 1-2 also shows that less than a majority of whites would vote for an open housing law that "says that a homeowner cannot refuse to sell to someone because of their color." Presumably the majority would vote for the version wherein "a homeowner can decide for himself." Apparently it matters little to the quarter of the white population who would restrict blacks from living in their neighborhood or the majority of respondents who would circumvent such restrictive covenants via a series of individual decision that the courts have long ruled such measures to be both illegal and actionable (i.e., the offended blacks can litigate to recover damages–including pain and suffering).

Not much change in racial attitudes is expected among white citizens in the near future because whites do not indicate a willingness to choose interracial contact. Contemporary surveys of whites indicate a reluctance to live with black neighbors, a desire to insulate themselves from contact with black people, and a desire to maintain a social distance from black Americans even while agreeing to formal legal and civil rights for black citizens. This suggests an insularity at the core of Euro-Americans racial attitudes that may persist for some time. Such conclusions imply an even greater imperative for legal interpretation and government enforcement to promote equal justice and to move towards the breaking up of systems of white domination.

## Table 1-2

Public Policy-Oriented Racial Attitudes, 1963-1986[a]

Percent of White Respondents[b]

| Survey Year | Disagree That Blacks Should Intrude | Disagree w/Black "Rights" to a Segregated Neighborhood | Would Vote for Open Housing Law | Favor Busing |
|---|---|---|---|---|
| 1963 | 22.3 | 44.9 | --- | --- |
| 1966 | 21.9 | --- | --- | --- |
| 1968 | 20.6 | 43.2 | --- | --- |
| 1970 | 15.6 | 50.6 | --- | 13.5 |
| 1971 | ---[c] | --- | --- | 17.8[d] |
| 1972 | 31.9[d] | 59.2[d] | --- | 19.5 |
| 1973 | 26.0 | --- | --- | 34.1 |
| 1974 | --- | --- | --- | 20.1 |
| 1975 | 24.8 | --- | 34.0 | 17.2 |
| 1976 | 28.5 | 59.6 | 34.6 | 15.8 |
| 1977 | 26.5 | 55.9 | --- | 16.3 |
| 1978 | --- | --- | 36.8 | 20.2 |
| 1980 | 31.1 | 64.8 | 38.8 | --- |
| 1982 | 39.3 | 70.2 | --- | 19.2 |
| 1983 | --- | --- | 44.4 | 23.1 |
| 1984 | 39.9 | 71.7 | 48.7 | --- |
| 1985 | 38.2 | 72.3 | --- | 22.0 |
| 1986 | --- | --- | 47.1 | 29.4 |

[a] All surveys conducted by the American Institute of Public Opinion (Gallup) or the National Opinion Research Center (NORC). All sampling errors ≤ 5%. See text for actual question wordings.
[b] Over 96.2% of all nonblack respondents are white.
[c] The dashed line indicates that this issue did not appear in any survey during this particular year.
[d] This is the mean response from two or more surveys that asked this question in this year.

Source: Racial Insularity at the Core: Contemporary American Racial Attitudes, by A. Wade Smith, 1988, Trotter Review, 2 (2) p. 11, Boston, MA: University of Massachusetts, William Monroe Trotter Institute.

## Value Orientations of Blacks

Stratification by race in America has also influenced the development of values among African-Americans (Himes, 1974). Here, care should be taken–heeding the admonitions of Ellison–not to equate all value orientations among black people as reactions to white domination. The complex relations between the dominant white American culture and the black American subculture creates a variety of sources for the development of social values among African-Americans. Scholars categorize these sources under two typologies: the traditional American value heritage, and ideological orientations within black communities. While more work needs to be done on regional variations, rural orientations, and relationships between the two major types, four categories of value orientations have been identified within urban black communities: (1) socially integrated, (2) structurally integrated, (3) structurally isolated, and (4) the excluded sector (Himes, 1987).

Black people who evidence socially integrated values generally maintain contact with black churches, social clubs, and voluntary associations, even though these are primarily oriented toward the values of the white communities where they live. They wish to be "Americans" in the general sense, although the degree to which this means that they wish to be assimilated as "white" Americans is not clear. Individuals of this orientation are success-oriented, and they demonstrate little support or empathy for confrontational racial protests. Members of these black families develop racially self-directed and self-maintaining values at the same time as they develop civil rights and public-policy values for use in the larger, white, bureaucratic, formal world. Black families in this category who live and work in desegregated areas tend to equip themselves to live in two different social worlds.

Members of the structurally integrated category work and sometimes live in integrated settings. Most, however, live–and all of them socialize–in a segregated world. Those who live in black neighborhoods do so because they want it that way. They evidence a split value system. On the one hand they live and work by general "white" American values. At the same time, they articulate well-known black values: that "black is beautiful"; that black history is an important part of their heritage; that black English is acceptable; and that black people are as intelligent and capable as white people. Additionally, they exhibit vigorous civil rights and public-policy values.

Black people in the structurally isolated category are generally employed in low-skilled and service sectors of the economy. The class system in the United States isolates these citizens. The economic and work values of those who are structurally isolated are developed through jobs where workers tend to feel cheated and oppressed by those in control. Therefore, the orientation of these black people is not toward traditional values but toward communal and ideological values of black communities, although some of the traditional values of the group coincide with those of the dominant American values (i.e., values of Southern black culture and black church culture). Blacks in this category tend to advocate the self-regarding and self-maintenance values of popular black culture. They acknowledge the importance of black history, culture, and society. Black English is legitimized and black heroes and heroines are idolized. These values sustain the sense of self-worth, boost morales, and serve to legitimize the cause of black people in the white-dominated society. Other value orientations among this group emphasize liberation, creative expression, and achievement. They support civil rights legislation and enforcement as well as the expansion of those gains already made. Collective action and confrontation are viewed as legitimate ways to pursue the struggle for black rights.

Members of the excluded sector are at the bottom of society in terms of economic and social indices. They are marginally employed or unemployed. They have little education and few marketable skills. Black people in this category are ill-housed, excluded from participation in the larger community, and alienated from the general society. Communications are generally broken with family, church, schools, media, and service agencies. Street life, the primary source of the development of values, does not function well to communicate and transmit traditional American values. In any case, many traditional values and social rules are ineffective in the real worlds that these people inhabit. Families in this grouping who stay in tune with traditional values are the exceptions.

Where do values come from in this grouping? They are improvised, borrowed, and developed pragmatically. Traditional values come to be viewed in pejorative and threatening terms. Indigenous values and norms are legitimized and enforced. There is evidence of hostility towards those in white communities as well as suspicion and distrust of white authority, especially the police. Members of this category exhibit support for civil rights efforts.

Elijah Anderson's work on marginally employed or unemployed black men in Chicago suggests a slightly different interpretation. According to Anderson, there are special hangouts in the cities that serve as gathering places for the urban poor and working-class people who seek a sense of self-worth and status through their sociability and interaction with peers. Urban taverns and bars, barbershops, carryouts, and their adjacent street corners and alleys are examples of the places that serve similar functions for the poor as more formal social clubs or domestic circles do for the middle and upper classes (Anderson, 1978).

Those who frequent these places create their own local, informal, social stratification system. Status within this system is action-oriented and precarious, based in large measure upon what people think and say and do about other members of the group. Extended primary groups develop in these places. Among the groups studied by Anderson the primary values were a "visible means of support" and "decency" (1978, p. 209). Residual values or values group members adopt after the "props" supporting decency have been judged to be unattainable or unavailable are "toughness," "gettin' big money," "gettin' some wine," and "having some fun."

Some writers have attempted to explain "low-class" values as weak imitations or approximations of the wider society's values. Rodman (1963), for example, has suggested that low-income people are unable to meet the larger society's standards of social conduct and therefore must stretch their own values to adjust to their particular life circumstances. Although there may be a certain amount of truth to this view, and it is supported by my own analysis, I believe it does not go far enough in appreciating the lives of the people involved and the internal coherence and integrity of their local stratification systems. The people I studied... appear not so much to "stretch" a given set of values to meet some general standard as to *create their own particular standards of social conduct* [emphasis added] along variant lines open to them. (Anderson, 1978, p. 210)

While this brief attempt to categorize black value orientations does not cover the entire spectrum of attitudes and values to be found among African-Americans, what is clear is that racial domination and the subordinate position of black Americans in society do influence the values espoused by black people as well as white people. The duality of values held are reminiscent of the concept of "twoness" employed by W.E.B. Du Bois in his 1903 book, *The Souls of Black Folk*. Interestingly, the reality of black peoples' lives, even for those who are classified as socially integrated, is one in which individuals and families exist in two different worlds, two different cultures, between which they must negotiate their existence.

## Scientific Racism[1]

There are in the dominant culture a number of mechanisms that reinforce and support white domination. These include ideologies of white supremacy. The most blatant contemporary ideological rationale for white domination is scientific racism. Scientific racism is rooted in the idea that domination is a right of the biologically superior. Scientific racism has produced "evidence" sustaining the belief that black people are inherently inferior, thus, rationalizing white rule.

The proponents of scientific racism advance arguments like those advocated by Social Darwinists earlier in this century. They argue for an educational system that will train the intellectually inferior for specific positions in the labor force. Also, again like the Social Darwinists, advocates of scientific racism view intelligence and achievement as products of innate genetic or cultural endowment. The logic of this has significant and potentially dangerous implications for social policy. If intelligence, achievement, mobility, and success are the products of inherent biological or cultural differences that cannot be altered by environment, then it is folly to try to alter social structures or institutional practices to promote equality or equal opportunity. Scientific racism goes further than Social Darwinism in not only blaming the victim but also in providing a quantitative and quasi-scientific basis for perpetuating inequality and domination.

Traits presumed to be biologically determined become the basis for social policy. This substantially limits the opportunities for targeted groups and makes them the victims of exclusion, sometimes even of extermination. In this century, Nazi Germany is associated with the most developed and horrifying application of social policy based on ideas of scientific racism. Here in the United States, prominent writers and scholars have contributed to the development of this phenomena, especially during the 1920s and 1930s. From the turn of the century through the 1930s scientific racism gained popularity in the United States in scholarly and popular literature. The enactment of the 1924 restrictive immigration bill may have been the highwater mark of the influence of these ideas during that period.

From the 1930s until the 1960s scientific racism was dormant. Now, however, the arguments have been resurrected in new forms. Gone are the archaic notions of phrenology and craniology that assumed that human worth and behavior could be determined by body type. Contemporary theorists seek instead to prove the primacy of heredity over environment in the determination of intelligence. The language is new, but the message is the same: genetic endowment is the great divider between superior and inferior types. Such differences cannot be mediated through legislation or social policy. Hence, racial differences are an immutable fact that are ordained genetically.

Scientific racism has functioned as an influence on public action. Such perceptions of human differences are a convenient *raison d'etre* for a stratified society. Some of the earliest theorists of the ideology of scientific racism were social scientists (Hofstadter, 1959; Schwendinger and Schwendinger, 1974). Preoccupied with social order and progress, they framed questions of individual and social difference as political questions. Their ideas, like all pseudo-scientific ideas regarding the human species, found acceptance among those seeking to justify the subordination of others. In periods of major social change such ideas tend to intensify as status positions are challenged. The 1960s was such a period.

The *Brown* decision (1954) altered the legal status of African-Americans and proved to be a catalyst for the modern civil rights movement. The court's ruling also struck at the core of the ideology of scientific racism. The philosophy of separate but equal had existed under the assumption of biological differences. Thus the ideology of scientific racism had given support to those who sought to maintain entitlement and privilege.

Scientific racism sees entitlement as a just reward to those who are genetically superior. Conversely, genetic inferiority is seen as the basis for restricting entitlement and privilege. Because of the presumptions about the association between race and superiority and inferiority, race becomes the key variable in restricting or granting entitlement. Members of the white race, designated by the ideology as biologically superior, are thus entitled to a superordinate status and the social, economic, and political privileges that are accorded this status. Members of the black race, designated by the ideology as biologically inferior, are denied any entitlement and privileges and are relegated to a subordinate status.

The *Brown* decision was a critical turning point not only in education but in the larger society because it set the stage for major alterations in the system of entitlement. The court's decision not only called into question the denial of choice in education, but also suggested a tolerance for a realignment in the historic patterns of power. The sociopolitical movements of the 1950s and 1960s vigorously sought such a realignment in the patterns of power relations, challenging the entitlements and privileges historically bestowed on white Americans.

The reemergence of the ideology of scientific racism during the past two decades has taken the form of an attack on the mental capacity of black children–and, by implication, all black people–by means of a dubious and abusive interpretation of intelligence testing. Arthur Jensen at the University of California at Berkeley, William Shockley of Stanford, and Richard Herrnstein of Harvard were in the forefront of a debate over the education of black children, the use of intervention strategies, and the development of public policy options to limit population growth among "genetically inferior blacks." All of these concepts were based on presumptions that intelligence was 80% inherited and 20% environment. Thus, policies that tried to use public funds or initiatives to improve the education and performance of black children were deemed to be undemocratic because they granted the disadvantaged some unearned privilege.

The proponents of scientific racism ignored evidence of historical, social, and structural influences on intelligence testing and ignored the decline in SAT scores among white students as well. The emphasis on quantitative data, performed in an advocacy manner, was an attempt to give the resurfaced ideology of white supremacy an aura of scientific objectivity and respectability. The appeal to the inheritability of intelligence restates the same argument that social classes are products of differential genetic stock. Scientific racism is an attempt to make inferiority a matter of science rather than prejudice.

W.E.B. Du Bois identified science and empire as the preeminent values in Western societies at the turn of the century (Du Bois, 1968). It should come as little surprise, then, that science during this century has been enlisted to justify political domination. The ideology of scientific racism has been invoked, in its least harmful form, as a rationalization for the insulation of privilege, the restraint of mobility, and the limitation of entitlement. In its most virulent form, scientific racism is a prescription for genocide.

The history of scientific racism is indicative of how data that purports to be "objective" may be used to promote reprehensible policy. Scientific racism has justified the deaths of countless millions of people by validating the claim that they were inferior and undeserving. A version of this ideology is being used today to justify the continuation of white domination and privilege.

## Racial Antagonism and Violence

In a racially stratified society, racial violence is used as a method of social control to maintain the structures of subordination. In a conspicuously violent society so stratified, violence is used for political purposes to maintain a racially bifurcated system, controlled politically by whites.

Historically, patterns of racial violence in the United States have moved in cycles of latent and aggressive activity. Latent periods have been relatively benign. During these periods the superordinate-subordinate system of race relations has been characterized by a kind of white paternalism. Aggressive periods have ensued when the system of domination has been challenged and/or the benefits of white superordination have been perceived to be eroding. During these periods, aggression and violence have been used to terrorize black people; the foundations of racial progress built by blacks have become targets for attack. The ebb and flow of racial violence has followed shifts in the national political economy and changing patterns in the labor force and the labor markets.

All institutions in American society have been permeated by the stratified and segmented nature of race relations. Racially motivated violence is a legacy of these unequal race relations, and it is endemic to the national political culture. Although manifest throughout American history, racial violence has differed in form and significance, breadth, and intensity from period to period.

This racially segmented social structure, established and maintained by violence, generates both systematic oppression of nonwhite racial groups, especially African-Americans, and systematic privileges for whites. The system of white privilege provides the philosophical and material basis for racism among whites. These privileges are the "white rights" that those who perpetuate racial violence are dedicated to defending.

White supremacy and racial oppression have been major factors in the political and economic development of this nation. The function of racial violence has been to establish and to perpetuate this system of differential privilege and deprivation based on race. Racial violence is a deliberate activity that reinforces ideologies of racial supremacy and intimidates the victims of violence and racial oppression.

Racial violence is currently on the upturn, a reaction to at least two important social dynamics: (1) the dramatic changes brought about by progress in civil rights; and (2) the dramatic transformations in the infrastructure of national economic life that have generated (since the Great Depression) unprecedented levels of unemployment, poverty, homelessness, and social dislocation. Currently, large segments of the American population are experiencing a heightened sense of insecurity and vulnerability.

Historically, racism has had the force of legal sanction. The legal system was key to the structuring of the system of white supremacy and racial oppression in the country. The slave codes, black codes, immigration laws, Indian treaties, and Jim Crow system explicitly constructed a "color line" and made racism the undisputed law of the land. Such laws, with the support of the Supreme Court in landmark decision like *Dred Scott* (1857) and *Plessy v. Ferguson* (1896) and a host of other lesser known but important rulings in Federal Appellate, state and county courts, detailed the structure of the racist status quo in practically all fields of social life from the labor market to housing, from schools to churches, from politics to social organizations.

The present rise of racist violence can best be understood in the context of the broad antiracist social movements in the 1960s and the early 1970s. Agencies of the government, as well as nongovernmental organizations, resorted to violence as a general tactic of intimidation in an endeavor to resist, slow down, and ultimately destabilize the movement's political assault on racism wholesale in society. This period was the occasion for large scale, frequent, racially motivated violence as the racists conducted open warfare against the black community. Hundreds of churches were bombed, thousands of people assaulted and banned from employment, dozens of civil rights workers wounded and murdered, including the assassination of Jimmy Young, Mack Parker, Medgar Evers, Viola Liuzzo, Bobby Hutton, Fred Hampton, Malcolm X, and Martin Luther King, to name but a few.

The racial violence of the 1960s was an extension of the common practice of lynching, which was still fairly active throughout the 1940s and during the 1950s, even after it had been formally outlawed. The two decades of the post-World War II era were characterized by racially organized terror against the black community, particularly in the South. This reign of terror was responsible, in part, for the migration of hundreds of thousands of people out of the South. But in the face of this adversity, the civil rights struggles produced a mass antiracism resistance movement for democratic rights. As a popular coalition it was able to obtain legal victories that virtually destroyed the legal, if not political, basis of racism.

By the early 1970s, the black political movement had successfully compelled the government to adopt affirmative action and desegregation policies that dictated positive action against racial dualism. However, it was precisely this antiracist political and ideological momentum that some conservative movements, including the "new right" as well as the white nationalists, began to organize to reverse. Racist violence is a part of this counter-attack. As in the past, racist violence is central to the effort to politically intimidate "minority" persons.

During the past decade several research centers have collected information on racially motivated violence.[2] A study of the data reveals an upsurge of racism and racist violence, with the most deadly attacks coming against the African-American community. There has been an increase in the number of incidents of white mobs attacking blacks in segregated residential areas. There has also been a steady increase in the fire-bombing of homes purchased by black families in predominately white neighborhoods. A study of violence in residential neighborhoods conducted by the Southern Poverty Law Center indicates that between 1985 and 1986 there were at least 45 cases of vigilante activity directed at black families who were moving into predominantly white communities. In the last five years incidents of racial harassment or violence have been reported on over 300 college campuses (Wilkerson, 1990).

The events in Howard Beach that led to the death of Michael Griffith in 1986 and the killing of Yusef Hawkins in Bensonhurst in 1989 reflect a long-standing problem of racist violence in white communities in New York City. Racially motivated assaults had increased to at least one a week in 1987. The Chicago Police Department reported a 58% increase in racial attacks for the first six months of 1986 over the same period in 1985. The New York City Police Department reported an increase in racially motivated violence over the last eight years. These attacks go mostly unreported in the news media.

The Community Relations Service of the Justice Department and the Center for Democratic Renewal ("Hate and Violence," 1987) provide data that demonstrate a sharp upturn nationally in violent racial attacks. The increase was 42% between 1985 and 1986, fueled largely by the boldness of white terrorist groups in the United States. Nationally, the Community Relations Services of the Justice Department reports an increase in all cases of racial confrontations from 953 in 1977 to 1,996 in 1982. The Justice Department also reported a 460% increase in cases of racial violence involving the Ku Klux Klan between 1978 and 1979, and a startling 550% increase in the period 1978 to 1980 (Walters, 1987).

The Ku Klux Klan has re-emerged with vigor. The Klan has always functioned as the armed militia for white supremacy. In his study of the civil rights movement in the South, Bloom gives a penetrating view of the Klan (1987):

> The Ku Klux Klan was an instrument of the struggle. All classes in the white South appear to have been involved in it and to have used it for different purposes. In the predominately white counties, which were usually located in the hills away from the fertile plantation areas, the Klan was used to drive Blacks out so as to eliminate them as competitors with white laborers... the upper class used the Klan to control Black labor, even to the detriment of white labor. Blacks who tried to leave the area were threatened with murder, and some of them were killed. When they did leave, they were sometimes dragged back, even across state lines...."These bands are having a great effect, in inspiring a nameless terror among Negroes, poor whites and others." (p. 4)

What was most important in winning upper-class support for the Klan was its political character. It is clear that the Klan did not emerge because of confusion in the South. It was founded for a very conscious and specific purpose: to defend slavery and racism and to defeat Reconstruction and civil rights. The Klan has never disappeared; and the Klan is a major factor in the rising racist violence of the present period. There were more Klan rallies in the period 1978-1980 than in the rest of the 1970s. The Klan burst on the national scene again in 1979 with a planned rifle attack on participants at an anti-Klan rally in the heart of the city of Greensboro, North Carolina, in broad daylight and in full view of local television cameras and reporters. In the 1980s their activities spread to Chicago, Ohio, New Jersey, Pennsylvania, as far north as Vermont, Maine and other northeast areas, and west to Colorado and California. Of course, the Klan is much smaller in size than it was years ago; and their strategies have also changed. The modern Klan seeks to shed the image of the night-rider vigilante for the role of street-level community organizer, where they motivate and direct alienation and anger in lower- and working-class white communities.

The question that begs consideration in an analysis of the rise of racism is what occasioned the resurgence of the racist in the mid-1970s? What is apparent is that the period 1973-1975 was the beginning of the deep recession cycles that narrowed the labor-market and set the economy in a state of stagnation that produced a decrease in the national standard of living. The contraction of the job market since the mid-1970s has produced an atmosphere of severe competition among workers. The steady shift of manufacturing outside the shores of the United States is forcing thousands of blue-collar workers to accept lower wages, seek new occupations, or be without employment altogether. Unemployment has been at record levels over the past decade. Not since the Great Depression of the 1930s has a generation of young working-class whites faced a future in which many can expect to earn and own less than their parents. The farm region is also experiencing a long-term depression with record foreclosures on family farmers brought on by trade deficits and monopolization of agribusiness and banks. This economic instability has produced a veritable sociological crisis for millions of working-class and farm families. They feel disavowed and disempowered.

In its 1980 annual report, the U.S. Justice Department makes the following observation (Walters, 1987):

> A factor for much of the racial and ethnic hostility was the perception by many white Americans that minorities, mainly blacks and Hispanics, were getting a better deal than anyone else, and that attention and continued effort to bring them into the mainstream threatened their welfare.

The ideology of the racist right focuses on the resentment felt in white communities. They orchestrate a "politics of resentment" by manipulating the issues of law and order, drugs, the death penalty, and affirmative action. In this climate, explicitly racist organizing has become widespread.

## Racial Change Since the 1960s

As a result of the Civil Rights Act of 1964 and the Voting Rights Act of 1965, the decade of the 1960s was a time of significant change in race relations in the United States. Consequently, it is a good reference point from which to begin an examination of trends and developments in the status of African-Americans. However, because racial change has been uneven, it is not possible to concisely summarize its direction over the past two decades.

The greatest changes have taken place in the political sphere. Black mayors are leading–or have led–all of the largest cities in the United States; and they preside over many medium-size cities as well. Although this has often entailed administering central cities burdened with well-nigh unsolvable problems within the context of a dominant white power structure, the new black political influence has also, on the plus side, democratized access to municipal and public service jobs.

The rise in black elected officials has been spectacular: the number increased from 280 in 1965 to 6,681 by 1987 (Boamah-Wiafe, 1990). Yet the fact that that figure represents less than 1.5% of all political officeholders shows that the degree of underrepresentation remains as significant as the gains (Joint Center for Political Studies, 1985).

Discrimination in jobs and training programs has definitely lessened over the past two decades. Yet racially exclusive practices still exist. Many small-sized firms (the fastest growing segment of the economy) exclude blacks and other minorities. And while affirmative action regulations constrain larger companies from such direct discrimination, ways are still found to insure predominantly white work forces–for example, by avoiding areas of large black populations in the location of plants.

These economic developments have had adverse effects on the integrity and unity of the black community. The nuclear family has been weakened by joblessness and by the single-parent trend. The extended family is no longer strong enough to fill the gap as successfully as it did in the past. Drugs and crime also divide the community, creating a climate of fear and distrust. Even in street life there is less solidarity than in the past. The increasing distance between the classes makes it harder for the community to act with a unified voice. And integration, with all its positive features, has also weakened the traditional institutions of the black community: black businesses, black colleges, and even the black church.

Some observers have lamented what they call the "loss of African-American community." Some of this loss can be attributed to the economic bifurcation of the community and the resulting loss of community infrastructure. In addition, there has been a significant loss of black principals, vice-principals, guidance counselors, teachers, and coaches, as a result of school desegregation. Usually, desegregation has meant that blacks have moved into white-dominated institutions, and the schools they left have been reassigned to other purposes or closed. Seldom has it meant that whites integrated into institutions that have been traditionally black and where blacks hold some of the power and influence.

## Conclusion

Significant changes have occurred in the racial landscape of America during the past 30 years. However, the basic structural position of African-Americans is the same. Prospects for improving this situation may be significantly affected by impressions held by white Americans about the status of black Americans. Most whites believe that blacks are approaching parity in areas like housing, health care, employment, education, and treatment by the criminal justice system–a perception markedly different from that of most blacks.

In a NAACP Legal Defense Fund study (1989), more than two-thirds of blacks, as compared with one-third of whites, felt that blacks had fewer employment opportunities than whites of similar income and education. In answer to the question of whether blacks received equal pay for equal work, whites responded yes more than twice as often as blacks. Two-thirds of blacks felt that blacks had poorer housing and less access to housing, while only 41% of whites felt that way; twice as many whites as blacks thought that blacks were treated as well as whites by the criminal justice system. As the NAACP Legal Defense Fund study concluded, these gaps in perception–and between perception and reality–need to be addressed by the nation's leaders. These opposing views regarding the parity of blacks and whites in society present a significant impediment to racial progress.

## Notes

1. This section is based on W. Edwards, (1988), Scientific Racism: Persistence and Change, *Trotter Institute Review*, 2 (3), 14-18, published by the William Monroe Trotter Institute, University of Massachusetts, Boston.

2. Including the Southern Poverty Law Center, The Center for Democrats Renewal, the Klan Watch Network, the Joint Center for Political Studies, and the Newsletter on Racially Motivated Violence.

## References

Anderson, E. (1978). *A Place on the Corner*. Chicago: University of Chicago Press.

Baldwin, J. (1985). Lecture. First Baptist Church of America, Providence, RI.

Bell, D.A. (1980a). *Civil Rights: Leading Cases*. Boston: Little Brown.

Bell, D.A. (1980b). *Race, Racism, and American Law* (2nd ed.). Boston: Little Brown.

Bloom, J.M. (1987). *Class, Race and the Civil Rights Movement*. Bloomington, IN: Indiana University Press.

Blumer, H. (1958). Race Prejudice as a Sense of Group Position. *Pacific Sociological Review, 1*, 3-7.

Boamah-Wiafe, D. (1990). *The Black Experience in Contemporary America*. Omaha: Wisdom Publications.

Bobo, L. (1983). Whites' Opposition to Busing: Symbolic Racism or Realistic Group Conflict? *Journal of Personality and Social Psychology, 45*, 1196-1210.

*Brown v. Board of Education*, 347 U.S. 483 (1954).

Clark, K. (1965). *Dark Getto*. New York: Harper and Row.

Cross, T.L. (1984). *The Black Power Imperative* (Rev. ed.). New York: Faulkner Books.

Danielson, M. (1976). *The Politics of Exclusion*. New York: Columbia University Press.

Dolce, P.C. (Ed.). (1976). *Suburbia*. New York: Doubleday.

*Dred Soctt v. Sanford*, 19 Howard 393 (60 U.S.) (1857).

Du Bois, W.E.B. (1961). *The Souls of Black Folk*. Greenwich, CT: Fawcett. (Originally published 1903).

Du Bois, W.E.B. (1968). *Dusk of Dawn: An Essay Toward an Autobiography of Race Concept*. New York: Schocker Books. (Originally published 1940).

Ellison, R. (1964). *Shadow and Act*. New York: Vintage.

Farley, R. (1970). The Changing Distribution of Negroes within Metropolitan Areas: The Emergence of Black Suburbs. *American Journal of Sociology, 75*, 512-519.

Feagin, J.R. & Feagin C. (1986). *Discrimination American Style*. Malabar, FL: Krieger Publishing.

Hate and Violence Mark 1986. (1987, March). *The Monitor*, p.1.

Himes, J. (1974). *Racial and Ethnic Relations*. Dubuque, IA: Brown.

Himes, J. (1987). Paper prepared for the Assessment of the Status of African-American Project, William Monroe Trotter Institute, University of Massachusetts, Boston.

Hofstadter, R. (1959). *Social Darwinism in American Thought* (Rev. ed.). New York: G. Braziller.

Joint Center for Political Studies. (1985). *Black Elected Officials: A National Roster*. Washington, DC: Joint Center for Political Studies.

*Jones v. Mayer*, 392 U.S. 409 (1968).

Levitan, S. et al. (1973). *Still A Dream*. Washington, DC: Manpower and Policy Studies.

Kinder, D.R. & Sears, D.C. (1991). Prejudice and Politics: Symbolic Racism Versus Racial Threats to a Good Life. *Journal of Personality and Social Psychology, 40*, 414-431.

McConahay, J.B. & Hough, J.C. (1976). Symbolic Racism. *Journal of Social Issues, 32*, 23-45.

NAACP Legal Defense Fund. (1989). *The Unfinished Agenda on Race in America*. New York: Author.

National Committee Against Discrimination in Housing. (no date). *Guide to Fair Housing Law Enforcement*. Washington, DC: Author.

National Urban League. (1985). *The State of Black America*. New York: Author.

Orfield, G. (1981). *Toward a Strategy of Urban Integration: Lessons in School and Housing Policy from Twelve Cities*. New York: Ford Foundation.

*Plessy v. Ferguson*, 163 U.S. 537 (1896).

Reed, W.L. (1989). *African Americans and Social Policy in the 1990s* (Occasional Paper No. 17). Boston, MA: University of Massachusetts at Boston, William Monroe Trotter Institute.

Rodman, H. (1963). The Lower Class Value Stretch. *Social Forces, 42* (2), 205-215.

Schuman, H., Steeh, C. & Bobo, L. (1985). *Racial Attitudes in America: Trends and Interpretations.* Cambridge, MA: Harvard University Press.

Schwendinger, H. & Schwendinger, J. (1974). *The Sociologists of the Chair.* New York: Basic Books.

*Shelley v. Kramer*, 334 U.S. 1 (1948).

Smith, A.W. (1981). Tolerance of School Desegregation, 1954-77. *Social Forces, 59,* 1256-1274.

Smith, A.W. (1982). White Attitudes Towards Residential Integration. *Phylon, 43,* 349-362.

Smith, A.W. (1985). Cohorts, Education, and the Evolution of Tolerance. *Social Science Research, 14,* 205-225.

Smith, A.W. (1988). Racial Insularity at the Core: Contemporary American Racial Attitudes. *Trotter Institute Review, 2* (2). Boston, MA: University of Massachusetts, William Monroe Trotter Institute.

Struyk, R. (1976). *Urban Home Ownership.* Lexington, MA: Lexington Books.

Swinton, D.H. (1990). Racial Parity Under Laissez-Faire: An Impossible Dream. In W.A. Van Horne and T.V. Tonnesen (Eds.), *Race: Twentieth Century Dilemnas–Twenty-First Century Prognoses.* Madison, WI: University of Wisconsin, Institute on Race and Ethnicity.

Taeuber, K.E. & Taeuber A.F. (1972). *Negroes in Cities.* New York: Atheneum.

Taylor, W.L. (1984). Access to Economic Opportunity. In L.W. Dunbar (Ed.), *Minority Report.* New York: Pantheon.

U.S. Commission on Civil Rights. (1974). *Equal Opportunity in Suburbia.* Washington, DC: Government Printing Office.

U.S. Commission on Civil Rights. (1975). *Twenty Years After Brown: Equal Opportunity in Housing.* Washington, DC: Government Printing Office.

U.S. Commission on Civil Rights. (1983). *A Sheltered Crisis: The State of Fair Housing in the Eighties.* Washington, DC: Government Printing Office.

U.S. Department of Housing and Urban Development. (1979). *Measuring Discrimination in American Housing Markets.* Washington, DC: Office of Policy Development and Research.

U.S. Department of Housing and Urban Development. (1984). *Recent Evidence on Discrimination in Housing.* Washington, DC: Office of Policy Development and Research

U.S. National Advisory Commission on Civil Disorders. (1968). *Report of the National Commission on Civil Disorders.* New York: Bantam Books.

Walters, R. (1987, April). *White Nationalism in America.* Paper presented at annual meeting of the African Heritage Studies Association, New York, NY.

Wilhelm, S. (1987). Paper prepared for the Assessment of the Status of African-Americans Project, William Monroe Trotter Institute, University of Massachusetts at Boston.

Wilkerson, I. (1990, May 9). Racial Harassment Altering Blacks' Choices on Campus. *New York Times*, pp. 1, B10.

# 2

# Race and Inequality in the Managerial Age

## William Darity, Jr.

*The Negro's prosperity today, limited as it is, is based upon the foundation laid by an alien race that is not disposed to go out of its way to prepare for the economic existence of anyone else but itself; therefore our present prosperity, as far as unemployment goes, is purely accidental. It is as accidental today as it was during the war of 1914-18 when colored men were employed in different occupations not because they were wanted, but because they were filling the places of men of other races who were not available at that time. Negroes are still filling places, and as time goes on and the age grows older our occupations will be gone from us, because those for whom we fill the places will soon appear, and as they do we shall gradually find our places among the millions of permanent unemployed.*

Marcus Garvey writing in the 1920s
(Jacques-Garvey, 1977)

In 1970 Sidney Wilhelm published a provocative book entitled *Who Needs the Negro?* that advanced the thesis that a technological transformation toward automation in the United States would render blacks–first relied upon for their labor under slavery and thereafter as an industrial reserve–unnecessary. Wilhelm noted that European settlers temporarily needed Native Americans upon arrival here to teach them crop techniques and to serve as allies against rival colonial powers. But in the post-colonial period the immigrant populations, who were soon to define the character of being "American," began to exterminate the natives. Wilhelm saw the same pattern developing for blacks in the late twentieth century.

In his review of Wilhelm's book, Lloyd Hogan (1972) complained:

The [Wilhelm] theory is too vague and lacks the societal frame of reference correlated with a given configuration of technology. There is no definitive role assigned to the various social classes as these social classes emerge from, and acquire their characteristic signature from, the essential relations within the productive process. (p. 109)

Nearly two decades later, Wilhelm's disturbing thesis remains substantive, and its implications are unfolding with growing visibility. It also is now possible to meet Hogan's requirement for a more precise theory, to draw a sharp connection between the technological phenomena Wilhelm depicted and the evolution of American social relations. Special attention must be given to the importance of the transition that has taken place from capitalist to managerial society, a transition from the dominance of the captains of industry and finance to the increasing dominance of the intellectuals and intelligentsia. The change is manifest in the authority given to experts in social analysis, policy making, and management. Within this transition race and ethnicity continue to exercise decisive roles in dictating patterns of individual achievement and opportunity in the United States.

In particular, discrimination in its most encompassing sense continues to be operative. Although laws have been passed to make certain of such practices illegal, these laws have been largely circumvented, ignored, or gradually rolled back. In many instances the laws have not touched critical sites of discriminatory activity. To the extent that American society is intensely hierarchical, there is an incentive for members of ascriptively differentiated groups to coalesce and carve out occupational and status niches. Antidiscrimination laws certainly were not designed to level the hiearchical structure of U.S. society; hence the driving motive for discrimination as exclusion remains strong.

Alterations in the structure of the U.S. economy–associated with the social transformation from capitalism to managerialism–have meant that those with low skill levels have been barred from occupations where they once had access because of increased competition as these positions diminish or disappear. Discrimination, both anterior and interior to the point of employment, has also meant that large numbers of blacks are denied access to the newer occupations.

These are the circumstances that accompany justified concerns over the perpetuation of an American "underclass," disproportionately black, reproduced from generation to generation. This underclass is a consequence of social forces that are being unleashed as capitalism gives way to the managerial estate. These forces play out along the dimensions of class, race, and ethnicity, and they structure patterns of inequality in American society.

In addition to the persistent interracial gap between blacks and whites, there is also an intraracial gap in the circumstances of blacks themselves that also demands assessment. In a society with an increasingly bifurcated employment structure, where occupational growth is concentrated in low-wage, low-skilled jobs and in high-wage professional positions, the mass of blacks–to the extent that they find employment at all–are concentrated in the former set of jobs. This concentration aggravates the degree of polarization between the majority of blacks and the relatively small percentage of blacks who hold professional level positions.

## The Opening Gap

The gap between the general circumstances of the native black population of the United States (the descendants of Africans enslaved in the colonial era) and the Native Indian population and the general circumstances of the nonblack majority (the descendants of Europeans who migrated to this continent) is multidimensional, reaching far beyond differences in economic well-being. The gap directly influences prospects for the health and well-being of upcoming generations, the sustenance of the spiritual and moral fiber of a people. The gap persists in the face of a host of changes: dramatic social policy initiatives such as the New Deal and the Great Society, the civil rights movement, periods of war and peace, and periods of prosperity and depression. The annual ritual of inspection of various statistical measures to assess the extent of black "progress"–undertaken for example in the National Urban League's annual publication *The State of Black America*–obscures the fundamental tenaciousness and pervasiveness of the gap. For even when such measures suggest changes in the absolute position of native blacks, they do not demonstrate over the long run any changes in the relative position.

Moreover, such statistical measures only scratch the surface of the deep gulf that exists between blacks and nonblacks in the United States. The narrow focus on indices of material well-being inhibits any serious analysis of the broad historical processes that have brought black America to its present position and continue to dictate its trajectory.

There is a deep contradiction in the economics literature of the late 1970s and early 1980s regarding the post-civil rights economic progress of black America. When examined carefully this contradiction indicates the opposing courses charted by the black underclass and the black middle class. For example, in 1973 Richard Freeman declared that there had been dramatic progress in the 1950s and especially in the 1960s, bringing blacks markedly closer to parity with whites in earnings. In fact, Freeman hypothesized that the trend toward "convergence in economic position...suggests a virtual collapse in traditional discriminatory patterns in the labor market" (p. 67). Freeman's declaration set the tone for a decade of research.

But in 1983 Freeman set the tone for the next decade's research with a far more somber message:

> The 1970s was a period of severe economic plight for inner-city black youth that went beyond the worst nightmares of even pessimistic social analysts. Rates of unemployment of young black men rose to unprecedented levels; labor participation rates fell; and as a consequence the ratio of employment to population plummeted to extraordinarily low levels.

James Smith and Finis Welch (1989), while maintaining the position that blacks have made substantial strides economically over the past 40 years (due, they claim, to educational advance), conclude a recent paper with the following pessimistic note: "Unfortunately, there are also reasons for concern about the future, especially for the still large black underclass..." (p. 561).

In 1973 Freeman's attention was drawn to the elite strata of the black population and to evidence of its improved economic position–an improvement that directly led toward convergence in aggregate black-white earnings ratios. In 1983 Freeman's attention was drawn to the black underclass, whose economic position had stagnated, even deteriorated, since the civil rights revolution. In 1989 Smith and Welch see these two strata of the black population living economically disparate existences.

The intraracial gap is so visible and pressing that even black scholars who once stressed the homogeneity of the native black population now have shifted gears. In 1983 Kenneth Clark and John Hope Franklin introduced a Joint Center for Political Studies publication with the following observation:

> At least three societies exist in America today: the mainstream, the assimilated minorities, and the excluded. These three societies are separate and unequal and the disparities between them threaten to destroy the national fabric. (p. 1)

The black middle class, situated awkwardly among the "assimilated minorities," continues to dream of entering fully into "the mainstream." But the black underclass is too deeply situated amongst "the excluded" for such dreaming.

Freeman's 1973 reading of the aggregate data was peculiarly optimistic and inaccurate, but he was not alone in offering this rosy picture of the quickening pace of black economic progress. His claim in 1973 was that labor market discrimination against blacks had been all but eliminated as a result of government antidiscrimination legislation and enforcement of affirmative action in hiring. Other scholars took the position that discrimination in labor markets could not persist anyway, regardless of government action, since the "natural" forces of competition would eliminate such discrimination, leaving only individual productivity differences as the basic explanation for racial inequality along wage-earning lines.[1] Whether it was government action or private action that was eliminating discrimination, all scholars agreed that the alleged decline in discrimination pointed towards improvement in the black condition. They then sought to quantify this improvement.[2]

Most of the good news emanating from these sources has been narrowly based, centering mainly on movements in black-white male wage and income ratios. Smith and Welch jubilantly proclaimed in 1986 that "[in 1940] the typical black male worker earned only 43% as much as his white counterpart. By 1980 the average black man in the labor force earned 73% as much as the typical white man" (p. 1). And although these wage gains were particularly substantial for black males with less than ten years of work experience, they were enjoyed as well by all other categories.

All of this is consistent with the Welch-Smith "vintage" hypothesis that predicts that better-educated young black males entering the labor market and replacing older, less well-educated blacks will, over time, accelerate the rate of convergence of black-white skills and hence black-white male wages. Indeed, in terms of quantity of schooling measured by median years, the racial gap has closed (see table 2-1). But the question remains: Does that translate into lessening of differences in income, opportunity, health, and well-being?

It should go without saying that the economic situation of native blacks as a whole can in no way be sufficiently represented by shifts in the income and earnings

## Table 2-1

Median Years of Schooling of Head for Families with Head 25-Years-Old and Older, by Poverty Status and Race of Head, 1970-1984[a]

| Year | Male Head | | | | Female Head | | | |
|---|---|---|---|---|---|---|---|---|
| | Below Poverty | | Total | | Below Poverty | | Total | |
| | Black | White | Black | White | Black | White | Black | White |
| 1984 | 10.6[b] | 12.1 | 12.3 | 12.7 | 11.6 | 12.0 | 12.2 | 12.5 |
| 1981 | 9.4 | 11.5 | 12.2 | 12.7 | 11.4 | 12.0 | 12.1 | 12.4 |
| 1980 | 9.3 | 11.1 | 12.1 | 12.6 | 11.1 | 11.9 | 12.0 | 12.6 |
| 1979 | 8.8 | 10.4 | 12.1 | 12.6 | 11.1 | 11.6 | 12.0 | 12.4 |
| 1978 | 8.7 | 10.5 | 12.2 | 12.6 | 11.0 | 11.8 | 11.8 | 12.3 |
| 1977 | 8.5 | 10.0 | 12.0 | 12.6 | 10.8 | 11.6 | 11.6 | 12.3 |
| 1976 | 8.7 | 10.3 | 11.7 | 12.5 | 10.5 | 11.4 | 11.4 | 52.2 |
| 1975 | 7.9 | 9.4 | 11.1 | 12.5 | 10.5 | 10.8 | 11.2 | 12.2 |
| 1974 | 7.2 | 9.6 | 10.9 | 12.5 | 10.4 | 10.7 | 11.0 | 12.2 |
| 1973 | 7.2 | 8.9 | 10.6 | 12.4 | 10.1 | 11.1 | 10.7 | 12.1 |
| 1972 | 8.1 | 8.9 | 10.6 | 12.4 | 10.1 | 10.8 | 10.7 | 12.1 |
| 1971 | 7.2 | 8.8 | 10.2 | 12.3 | 9.9 | 10.4 | 10.3 | 12.1 |
| 1970 | 6.8 | 8.7 | 10.0 | 12.3 | 9.3 | 10.5 | 10.1 | 12.1 |

[a]Data in this series are unavailable between 1982 and 1983.
[b]In 1984, half of black male householders whose families had incomes below the poverty level had less than 10.6 years of schooling and half had more.

Source: U.S. Bureau of Census, *Current Population Reports, Consumer Income*, Series P-60, No. 81, pp. 83-84; No. 86, pp. 113-114; No. 91, pp. 113-114; No. 98, pp. 117-118; No. 102, p. 105; No. 105, p. 132; No. 115, p. 135; No. 119, p. 133; No. 124, p. 145; No. 130, p. 140; No. 133, p. 128; No. 149, pp. 28, 29. March 1982, *Current Population Survey*, (unpublished data), pp. 390, 392, 400, 398, 416, 414, 424, 422.

of black males relative to white males. There are other important indicators that must be considered in order to portray the past and present economic conditions of blacks. But even the picture with regards to black male income and earnings has clouded over since the 1970s when Welch and Smith last took an in-depth look. Bradbury and Browne (1986) have adduced evidence that shows not only a decline in the black-white male median income ratio since 1978, but also an apparent breakdown in the much-vaunted vintage effect.

Table 2-2 is an expanded and somewhat modified version of the Bradbury and Brown data. It can be seen there that the black-white median income ratio for fully employed males of all ages rose from .64 in 1967 to a high of .77 in 1978 and then fell to .68 in 1984. The incomes of younger black males, those 20 to 34 years of age, were generally higher relative to their white counterparts than those of older black males. The "average" black-white income ratio for 20- to 24-year-olds over the 18-year period was slightly over .79, while that for 25- to 34-year-olds was around .76. For 35- to 44-year-olds the average over the period was .69; for 45- to 54-year-olds it was .65; and for 55- to 64-year-olds it was .64. In accord with the expectations of the vintage hypothesis, younger blacks in the late 1960s with higher relative incomes than older cohorts were able to improve or at least maintain their relative income position over the next ten years.

In table 2-3, changes in the income ratios of various cohorts over ten-year time spans are shown. The 20- to 24-year-old cohorts of 1967 to 1970, and the 25- to 34-year-old cohorts of 1967 to 1969 either improved or held to their relative income positions over the next ten years. After 1980, however, as Bradbury and Browne state, "this positive ripple effect broke down" (1986, p. 34). With but one exception the relative incomes of the 20- to 24-year-old and 25- to 34-year-old cohorts of 1971 to 1974 had decreased ten years later over the 1981 to 1984 period. Black male workers who were 35 years and older in the late 1960s and mid-1970s also fared poorly over the next ten years. With but few exceptions their relative incomes were lower ten years later.

The ten-year span for the 20- to 24-year-old cohorts from 1970 to 1974 can be divided into two five-year periods. The slight increase in the relative income of the 20- to 24-year-old cohort between 1970 and 1980 was composed of a sharp rise between 1970 and 1975 and an almost equally sharp decline between 1975 and 1980. The 1973 cohort experienced an even steeper rise in their relative incomes between 1973 and 1978 and an even greater decline between 1978 and 1983. Nor were the 1980s kind to the 30- to 34-year-old and 35- to 39-year-old cohorts over the five-year spans beginning in 1975. The general picture suggested by this data does not support the predictions of those who argued that the wage gains experienced by black males in the late 1960s and early 1970s would be maintained throughout their work careers. Life-cycle "gains" are not borne out by the data.

# Table 2-2

Black-White Male Median Income Ratios for Year-Round,
Fully Employed Workers, by Age Cohorts, 1967-1987

| Year | All Ages[a] | 20-24 | 25-34 Total | 25-29 | 30-34 | 35-44 Total | 35-39 | 40-44 | 45-54 | 55-64 |
|---|---|---|---|---|---|---|---|---|---|---|
| 1967 | .64 | .68 | .73 | n.a. | n.a. | .61 | n.a. | n.a. | .65 | .57 |
| 1968 | .68 | .77 | .71 | n.a. | n.a. | .63 | n.a. | n.a. | .68 | .64 |
| 1969 | .66 | .80 | .70 | n.a. | n.a. | .66 | n.a. | n.a. | .66 | .62 |
| 1970 | .68 | .77 | .72 | n.a. | n.a. | .65 | n.a. | n.a. | .67 | .67 |
| 1971 | .68 | .86 | .73 | n.a. | n.a. | .63 | n.a. | n.a. | .66 | .60 |
| 1972 | .68 | .81 | .72 | n.a. | n.a. | .65 | n.a. | n.a. | .63 | .66 |
| 1973 | .67 | .79 | .76 | n.a. | n.a. | .68 | n.a. | n.a. | .64 | .62 |
| 1974 | .70 | .79 | .80 | n.a. | n.a. | .71 | n.a. | n.a. | .67 | .64 |
| 1975 | .73 | .83 | .80 | .85 | .75 | .72 | .75 | .69 | .68 | .71 |
| 1976 | .72 | .81 | .79 | .81 | .76 | .69 | .70 | .68 | .66 | .66 |
| 1977 | .69 | .84 | .75 | .77 | .76 | .74 | .72 | .75 | .69 | .60 |
| 1978 | .77 | .72 | .86 | .90 | .84 | .77 | .81 | .74 | .69 | .69 |
| 1979 | .73 | .79 | .78 | .77 | .80 | .76 | .77 | .75 | .65 | .66 |
| 1980 | .70 | .83 | .76 | .76 | .78 | .71 | .70 | .73 | .64 | .65 |
| 1981 | .71 | .82 | .78 | .82 | .76 | .68 | .66 | .69 | .61 | .66 |
| 1982 | .71 | .82 | .77 | .74 | .79 | .69 | .73 | .65 | .64 | .67 |
| 1983 | .71 | .74 | .75 | .75 | .75 | .76 | .80 | .75 | .67 | .60 |
| 1984 | .68 | .80 | .72 | .69 | .73 | .76 | .82 | .69 | .67 | .60 |
| 1985 | .70 | .79 | .73 | .69 | .70 | .70 | .72 | .69 | .68 | .68 |
| 1986 | .71 | .76 | .73 | .71 | .73 | .73 | .73 | .73 | .71 | .61 |
| 1987 | .71 | .79 | .71 | .75 | .69 | .76 | .75 | .78 | .66 | .65 |

[a]Includes persons 14 years and older in 1967-1978, and 15 years and older in 1979-1987.
Source: U.S. Bureau of Census, *Current Population Reports*, Series P-60, Money Income of Households, Families and Persons in the United States, various years.

## Table 2-3

Changes in Black-White Male Median Income Ratios Over
Various Time Spans, by Selected Age Cohorts, 1967-1987

| Year | 10-Year Span 20-24 | Year | 30-34 | Direction of change in ratios over time span |
|---|---|---|---|---|
| 1967 | .68 | 1977 | .76 | increase |
| 1968 | .77 | 1978 | .84 | increase |
| 1969 | .80 | 1979 | .80 | unchanged |
| 1970 | .77 | 1980 | .78 | increase |
| 1971 | .86 | 1981 | .81 | decrease |
| 1972 | .81 | 1982 | .79 | decrease |
| 1973 | .79 | 1983 | .73 | decrease |
| 1974 | .79 | 1984 | .73 | decrease |
| 1975 | .83 | 1985 | .69 | decrease |
| 1976 | .81 | 1986 | .71 | decrease |
| 1977 | .84 | 1987 | .69 | decrease |

| Year | 10-Year Span 25-34 | Year | 35-44 | Direction of change in ratios over time span |
|---|---|---|---|---|
| 1967 | .73 | 1977 | .74 | increase |
| 1968 | .71 | 1978 | .77 | increase |
| 1969 | .70 | 1979 | .76 | increase |
| 1970 | .72 | 1980 | .71 | decrease |
| 1971 | .73 | 1981 | .68 | decrease |
| 1972 | .72 | 1982 | .69 | decrease |
| 1973 | .76 | 1983 | .76 | unchanged |
| 1974 | .80 | 1984 | .76 | decrease |
| 1975 | .80 | 1985 | .70 | decrease |
| 1976 | .79 | 1986 | .73 | decrease |
| 1977 | .75 | 1987 | .76 | increase |

| Year | 10-Year Span 35-44 | Year | 45-54 | Direction of change in ratios over time span |
|---|---|---|---|---|
| 1967 | .61 | 1977 | .59 | decrease |
| 1968 | .63 | 1978 | .69 | increase |
| 1969 | .66 | 1979 | .65 | decrease |
| 1970 | .65 | 1980 | .64 | decrease |
| 1971 | .63 | 1981 | .63 | decrease |
| 1972 | .65 | 1982 | .64 | decrease |
| 1973 | .68 | 1983 | .67 | decrease |
| 1974 | .71 | 1984 | .67 | decrease |
| 1975 | .72 | 1985 | .68 | decrease |
| 1976 | .69 | 1986 | .71 | increase |
| 1977 | .74 | 1987 | .66 | decrease |

## Table 2-3 (continued)

| | 10-Year Span | | | Direction of change in ratios over time span |
|---|---|---|---|---|
| Year | 45-54 | Year | 55-64 | |
| 1967 | .65 | 1977 | .60 | decrease |
| 1968 | .68 | 1978 | .69 | increase |
| 1969 | .68 | 1979 | .65 | unchanged |
| 1970 | .67 | 1980 | .60 | decrease |
| 1971 | .66 | 1981 | .66 | unchanged |
| 1972 | .63 | 1982 | .67 | increase |
| 1973 | .64 | 1983 | .60 | decrease |
| 1974 | .67 | 1984 | .60 | decrease |
| 1975 | .68 | 1985 | .68 | unchanged |
| 1976 | .66 | 1986 | .61 | decrease |
| 1977 | .59 | 1987 | .65 | increase |

| | 5-Year Span | | | | |
|---|---|---|---|---|---|
| Year | 20-24 | Year | 25-29 | Year | 30-34 |
| 1970 | .77 | 1975 | .85 | 1980 | .78 |
| 1971 | .86 | 1976 | .81 | 1981 | .76 |
| 1972 | .81 | 1977 | .77 | 1982 | .79 |
| 1973 | .79 | 1978 | .90 | 1983 | .73 |
| 1974 | .79 | 1979 | .77 | 1984 | .73 |
| 1975 | .83 | 1980 | .76 | 1985 | .69 |
| 1976 | .81 | 1981 | .82 | 1986 | .71 |
| 1977 | .84 | 1982 | .74 | 1987 | .69 |
| 1978 | .72 | 1983 | .75 | | |
| 1979 | .79 | 1984 | .69 | | |
| 1980 | .83 | 1985 | .77 | | |
| 1981 | .82 | 1986 | .73 | | |
| 1982 | .82 | 1987 | .75 | | |

| | 5-Year Span | | | Direction of change in ratios over time span |
|---|---|---|---|---|
| Year | 30-34 | Year | 35-39 | |
| 1975 | .75 | 1980 | .70 | decrease |
| 1976 | .76 | 1981 | .66 | decrease |
| 1977 | .76 | 1982 | .73 | decrease |
| 1978 | .84 | 1983 | .80 | decrease |
| 1979 | .80 | 1984 | .82 | increase |
| 1980 | .78 | 1985 | .72 | decrease |
| 1981 | .76 | 1986 | .73 | decrease |
| 1982 | .79 | 1987 | .75 | decrease |

## Table 2-3 (continued)

| Year | 5-Year Span 30-39 | Year | 40-44 | Direction of change in ratios over time span |
|------|------|------|------|------|
| 1975 | .69 | 1980 | .73 | increase |
| 1976 | .70 | 1981 | .69 | decrease |
| 1977 | .82 | 1982 | .65 | decrease |
| 1978 | .81 | 1983 | .75 | decrease |
| 1979 | .77 | 1984 | .69 | decrease |
| 1980 | .70 | 1985 | .69 | decrease |
| 1981 | .66 | 1986 | .73 | increase |
| 1982 | .73 | 1987 | .78 | increase |

Source: See table 2-2.

Matters are further complicated by the fact that the basis for the numbers in tables 2-2 and 2-3 is a rather selective one and does not reflect the full reality of white male-black male income disparities. The data in tables 2-2 and 2-3 are based on year-round, full-time workers, and such workers among blacks are a smaller proportion of all income recipients than they are among whites. Moreover, while the proportion of full-time male workers has been declining for both groups, the decline in absolute terms for blacks has been greater than that for whites. In 1967, as table 2-4 shows, 53% of black male workers worked full-time year-round, while for white workers the figure was 61.5%. By 1987 the black male proportion was about 5 percentage points lower, and the white male proportion was down 6 percentage points to 56.5%. The lowest point was 41.5% for black males in 1982 and 51.9% for white males during the same year.

A more telling measure is the income ratio for all workers, both full- and part-time and full- and part-year. A comparison of the data in table 2-5 and that in table 2-2 shows that the absolute values of the median income ratios for all workers are lower than they are for full-time workers. Between 1967 and 1974, the average difference between the two ratios for workers of all ages was around 8%. Between 1975 and 1987 the average difference increased to around 12%. None of this affects the conclusions reached with respect to the decline in black relative incomes by age cohorts over the 1980s. Whether we use full-time data or part-time data the decline is still there.

A measure closer still to the economic reality of black males is that adopted by Darity, (1980; Darity & Myers, 1980) who included not only those with income but those without as well. This requires us to use mean rather than median as the measure of average and to correct it for those who have been excluded because they had no income.[3] This simple correction involves multiplying the mean by the proportion of the population with income. Such a result is presented in table 2-6. The proportion of black males with income declined slightly over the 1967-1987 period, while the proportion of whites with income increased. In contrast to the median income ratios in table 2-2, the mean income ratios are uniformly lower and the "corrected" mean income ratios lower still. Once again, the story is the same with respect to progress in this ratio. While the ratio for fully employed workers was higher in 1987 than in 1967 (.71 versus .64), and the ratio for all workers also was higher in 1987 than 1967 (.59 versus .57), the mean income ratio for those with and without income was an identical .55 in both years.

Expected payoffs in income relative to increased black male educational attainment also hit a snag during the 1980s. As table 2-7 shows, the black-white median income ratios for males 25 years and older in all schooling classes rose in the late 1960s and early 1970s. During the 1980s, however, the rates declined for all except those with four or more years of college. The decline was particularly pronounced among black high school graduates whose income relative to whites was the same in 1987 as in 1964. It would appear from this data that the relative income gains associ-

## Table 2-4

Year-Round, Full-Time Workers as a Percent of All Workers, 1967-1987

| Year | Black Males | White Males | Black Females | White Females |
|------|-------------|-------------|---------------|---------------|
| 1967 | 53.0% | 61.5% | 31.8% | 31.7% |
| 1968 | 53.0 | 61.1 | 31.2 | 31.0 |
| 1969 | 51.7 | 59.9 | 30.0 | 30.8 |
| 1970 | 50.0 | 57.3 | 30.6 | 29.9 |
| 1971 | 48.4 | 57.3 | 29.6 | 30.5 |
| 1972 | 50.8 | 58.2 | 32.8 | 30.3 |
| 1973 | 50.5 | 58.7 | 31.3 | 30.0 |
| 1974 | 46.7 | 56.9 | 30.4 | 30.3 |
| 1975 | 43.3 | 54.1 | 29.2 | 28.6 |
| 1976 | 45.2 | 54.1 | 29.7 | 28.5 |
| 1977 | 46.3 | 54.5 | 30.4 | 29.2 |
| 1978 | 45.0 | 55.9 | 31.4 | 28.8 |
| 1979 | 46.8 | 56.1 | 30.3 | 27.5 |
| 1980 | 43.8 | 55.0 | 31.4 | 27.9 |
| 1981 | 45.2 | 53.9 | 31.0 | 28.0 |
| 1982 | 41.5 | 51.9 | 32.0 | 28.3 |
| 1983 | 43.9 | 52.7 | 33.2 | 29.6 |
| 1984 | 44.8 | 54.9 | 35.0 | 30.3 |
| 1985 | 47.5 | 55.3 | 35.7 | 31.0 |
| 1986 | 46.4 | 55.3 | 35.3 | 31.8 |
| 1987 | 48.5 | 56.5 | 36.4 | 32.9 |

Source: See table 2-2.

## Table 2-5

### Black-White Male Median Income Ratios for All Workers, by Age Cohorts, 1967-1987

| Year | All Ages[a] | 20-24 | 25-34 | 35-44 | 45-54 | 55-64 |
|------|-------------|-------|-------|-------|-------|-------|
| 1967 | .57 | .71 | .72 | .56 | .57 | .53 |
| 1968 | .59 | .83 | .70 | .62 | .63 | .53 |
| 1969 | .58 | .91 | .65 | .62 | .57 | .56 |
| 1970 | .59 | .80 | .65 | .62 | .61 | .55 |
| 1971 | .60 | .78 | .68 | .58 | .61 | .54 |
| 1972 | .61 | .82 | .70 | .60 | .60 | .48 |
| 1973 | .61 | .84 | .71 | .61 | .57 | .53 |
| 1974 | .61 | .77 | .74 | .64 | .55 | .53 |
| 1975 | .60 | .81 | .73 | .63 | .53 | .53 |
| 1976 | .60 | .76 | .69 | .64 | .56 | .53 |
| 1977 | .59 | .78 | .70 | .66 | .53 | .52 |
| 1978 | .60 | .68 | .73 | .70 | .61 | .51 |
| 1979 | .63 | .75 | .72 | .63 | .56 | .51 |
| 1980 | .60 | .71 | .68 | .61 | .56 | .49 |
| 1981 | .60 | .76 | .70 | .66 | .56 | .47 |
| 1982 | .60 | .61 | .71 | .62 | .56 | .50 |
| 1983 | .58 | .54 | .65 | .66 | .62 | .52 |
| 1984 | .57 | .69 | .60 | .63 | .60 | .47 |
| 1985 | .63 | .62 | .69 | .64 | .63 | .53 |
| 1986 | .60 | .61 | .65 | .65 | .62 | .54 |
| 1987 | .59 | .63 | .65 | .66 | .56 | .51 |

[a]Includes persons 14 years and older in 1967-1978, and 15 years and older in 1979-1987.

Source: See table 2-2.

## Table 2-6

Mean Income for Males with and without Income, 1967-1987

| Year | Mean Income | Approximate Share | Black Mean Income | White Mean Income | Approximate Share | Corrected White Mean Income | Black-White Income Ratio | Corrected Black-White Income Ratio |
|---|---|---|---|---|---|---|---|---|
| 1967 | $3,696 | .88 | $3,260 | $6,414 | .93 | $5,956 | .59 | .55 |
| 1968 | 4,018 | .89 | 3,559 | 6,895 | .93 | 6,407 | .59 | .56 |
| 1969 | 4,361 | .88 | 3,857 | 7,508 | .93 | 6,984 | .58 | .55 |
| 1970 | 4,683 | .86 | 4,027 | 7,840 | .93 | 7,273 | .60 | .55 |
| 1971 | 4,888 | .86 | 4,182 | 8,203 | .92 | 7,583 | .60 | .55 |
| 1972 | 5,447 | .84 | 4,572 | 8,980 | .93 | 8,318 | .61 | .55 |
| 1973 | 5,864 | .86 | 5,057 | 9,652 | .93 | 9,004 | .61 | .56 |
| 1974 | 6,210 | .85 | 5,263 | 10,083 | .93 | 9,420 | .62 | .56 |
| 1975 | 6,633 | .84 | 5,549 | 10,832 | .93 | 10,025 | .61 | .55 |
| 1976 | 7,180 | .84 | 6,034 | 11,604 | .93 | 10,836 | .62 | .56 |
| 1977 | 7,743 | .84 | 6,513 | 12,537 | .93 | 11,659 | .62 | .56 |
| 1978 | 8,541 | .86 | 7,307 | 13,609 | .93 | 12,839 | .63 | .57 |
| 1979 | 9,383 | .88 | 8,279 | 14,920 | .96 | 14,376 | .63 | .58 |
| 1980 | 9,843 | .87 | 8,607 | 15,967 | .96 | 15,299 | .62 | .56 |
| 1981 | 10,531 | .87 | 9,119 | 17,195 | .96 | 16,507 | .61 | .55 |
| 1982 | 11,050 | .83 | 9,199 | 18,071 | .95 | 17,201 | .61 | .53 |
| 1983 | 11,501 | .84 | 9,716 | 18,823 | .95 | 17,941 | .61 | .54 |
| 1984 | 12,119 | .86 | 10,409 | 20,259 | .96 | 19,367 | .60 | .54 |
| 1985 | 13,376 | .87 | 11,678 | 21,523 | .96 | 20,569 | .62 | .57 |
| 1986 | 13,861 | .87 | 12,124 | 22,746 | .96 | 21,749 | .61 | .56 |
| 1987 | 14,391 | .87 | 12,500 | 23,643 | .96 | 22,691 | .61 | .55 |

Source: See table 2-2.

## Table 2-7

Black-White Male Median Income Ratios, by Educational Attainment, Persons 25 Years and Older, Selected Years

| Year | Elementary 0-8 Years | Some HighSchool 9-11 years | High School Grad 12 year | Total College 13+ years | Some College 13-15 years | College Plus 16+ years |
|---|---|---|---|---|---|---|
| 1964 | .67 | .68 | .66 | .66 | n.a. | n.a. |
| 1969 | .73 | .71 | .71 | .69 | .74 | .69 |
| 1974 | .68 | .74 | .76 | .73 | .78 | .71 |
| 1980 | .63 | .76 | .73 | .70 | .74 | .71 |
| 1984 | .68 | .71 | .66 | .69 | .74 | .71 |
| 1985 | .67 | .80 | .74 | .68 | .71 | .77 |
| 1986 | .63 | .81 | .71 | .70 | .77 | .73 |
| 1987 | .73 | .71 | .66 | .70 | .77 | .73 |

Source: See table 2-2.

ated with increased educational attainments made by black males during the 1960s and 1970s have eroded in the 1980s.

Finally, we consider measures of the relative resources available to the black family. Two such measures, median family income and family wealth and asset ownership, also belie the claims of "dramatic" black economic advances. In 1967, as table 2-8 shows, the average black family had an income of $15,166 (in 1984 dollars) available to it, whereas the average white family enjoyed an income that was $10,450 higher at $25,616. Thus for every $1 of white family income, black families had 59 cents. By 1984 the gap had grown wider. Black median family income in 1984 was $15,431, some $12,255 less than the $27,686 white families received. In that year, for every $1 of white family income black families had 56 cents. Moreover, white families fared much better than blacks in terms of real income growth. The black 1984 median family income was just $265 higher than the 1967 income; whites on the other hand enjoyed an increase of $2,070 over their 1967 income. And while black family income rose between 1967 and 1978, when it peaked at $17,321, so also did the difference rise between the amount of income available to whites and to blacks. This difference reached its peak in 1979 at $12,686. After 1978 and 1979, both black and white real income started to decline, but black income declined faster.

If one wishes to take a slightly longer view of racial income comparisons, one must use the "black and other races" category. Data on relative median family income for this category goes back to 1947. Although blacks make up the overwhelming majority of the families in this category, the income disparity between blacks and the other groups such as Chinese and Japanese is such that it lends a considerable upward bias to the ratio. In table 2-9, the two income ratios are presented and contrasted. It not only shows the degree of divergence between the two statistics, but also indicates that there has been an increase in this divergence over time. The 1967-1987 interval seems to be composed of two distinct periods. From 1967 to 1976 the average difference between the two ratios was 2.9%; but from 1977 to 1984 the difference almost doubled to 5.4%. It might be inferred from this that the other races in the category have been making substantial economic gains relative to blacks since 1977. However, even if one relied solely on the black-and-other/white ratio, things still would not look very rosy. The black-and-other/white ratio hovered between .51 and .57 from the 1940s, into the mid-1960s. Then it rose fitfully over the late 1960s and reached its peak of .65 in 1975. It has since headed downward and has been stuck at around .62 throughout the 1980s.

It is of interest to note how black relative family incomes have fared under different federal administrations. In table 2-10 such a comparison is made. Black family income was highest on average during the two Ford years, while the next highest period was during the six-year Nixon regime. Black relative family income was at its lowest during the first four Reagan years. During that time black families had on average $1,800 less in yearly income than they did during Ford the years. The story is exactly the same for the median income of blacks and other races during the 1967-1984 period, only the numbers are slightly higher.

## Table 2-8

### Black-White Median Family Income, in 1984 Dollars, 1967-1984

| Year | Black Median Income | White Median Income | White-Black Median Income Difference | Black-White Median Income Ratio |
|------|---------------------|---------------------|--------------------------------------|---------------------------------|
| 1967 | $15,166 | $25,616 | $10,450 | .59 |
| 1968 | 16,003 | 26,682 | 10,659 | .60 |
| 1969 | 16,997 | 27,750 | 10,753 | .61 |
| 1970 | 16,596 | 27,381 | 10,585 | .61 |
| 1971 | 16,517 | 27,371 | 10,854 | .60 |
| 1972 | 17,042 | 28,674 | 11,632 | .59 |
| 1973 | 16,990 | 29,439 | 12,449 | .58 |
| 1974 | 16,863 | 28,241 | 11,378 | .60 |
| 1975 | 16,943 | 27,536 | 10,593 | .62 |
| 1976 | 16,863 | 28,349 | 11,486 | .60 |
| 1977 | 16,391 | 28,693 | 12,302 | .57 |
| 1978 | 17,321 | 29,244 | 11,923 | .59 |
| 1979 | 16,562 | 29,248 | 12,686 | .57 |
| 1980 | 15,976 | 27,611 | 11,635 | .58 |
| 1981 | 15,151 | 26,858 | 11,707 | .56 |
| 1982 | 14,633 | 26,475 | 11,482 | .55 |
| 1983 | 15,181 | 26,937 | 11,756 | .56 |
| 1984 | 15,431 | 27,686 | 12,255 | .56 |

Source: See table 2-1.

## Table 2-9

Comparison of Black and Other Races-White Median Family Income Ratios and Black-White Median Family Income Ratios, 1947-1987

| Year | Black & Other Races-White Ratio | Black-White Ratio | Year | Black & Other Races-White Ratio | Black-White Ratio | Difference Between Ratios |
|---|---|---|---|---|---|---|
| 1947 | .51 | n.a. | 1967 | .62 | .59 | .03 |
| 1948 | .53 | n.a. | 1968 | .63 | .60 | .03 |
| 1949 | .51 | n.a. | 1969 | .63 | .61 | .02 |
| 1950 | .54 | n.a. | 1970 | .64 | .61 | .03 |
| 1951 | .53 | n.a. | 1971 | .63 | .60 | .03 |
| 1952 | .57 | n.a. | 1972 | .62 | .59 | .03 |
| 1953 | .56 | n.a. | 1973 | .60 | .58 | .02 |
| 1954 | .56 | n.a. | 1974 | .64 | .60 | .04 |
| 1955 | .55 | n.a. | 1975 | .65 | .62 | .03 |
| 1956 | .53 | n.a. | 1976 | .63 | .60 | .03 |
| 1957 | .54 | n.a. | 1977 | .61 | .57 | .04 |
| 1958 | .51 | n.a. | 1978 | .64 | .59 | .05 |
| 1959 | .52 | n.a. | 1979 | .61 | .57 | .04 |
| 1960 | .55 | n.a. | 1980 | .63 | .58 | .05 |
| 1961 | .53 | n.a. | 1981 | .62 | .56 | .06 |
| 1962 | .53 | n.a. | 1982 | .62 | .55 | .07 |
| 1963 | .53 | n.a. | 1983 | .62 | .56 | .06 |
| 1964 | .56 | n.a. | 1984 | .62 | .56 | .05 |
| 1965 | .55 | n.a. | 1985 | .64 | .58 | .06 |
| 1966 | .60 | n.a. | 1986 | .63 | .57 | .06 |
|  |  |  | 1987 | .63 | .56 | .07 |

Source: See table 2-2.

## Table 2-10

### Median Family Income During the Last Eight Administrations, in 1984 Dollars

| Administration[a] | Black Median Income | Black & Other Median Income | White Median Income | Black-White Ratio | Black & Other Races-White Ratio |
|---|---|---|---|---|---|
| Truman 1947-52    | n.a.   | $ 7,944 | $14,907 | n.a. | .53 |
| Eisenhower 1953-60 | n.a.   | 10,064  | 18,693  | n.a. | .54 |
| Kennedy 1961-63   | n.a.   | 11,421  | 21,466  | n.a. | .53 |
| Johnson 1964-66   | n.a.   | 13,671  | 23,961  | n.a. | .57 |
| Johnson 1967-68   | 15,585 | 16,269  | 26,149  | .60  | .62 |
| Nixon 1969-74     | 16,868 | 17,609  | 28,143  | .60  | .63 |
| Ford 1975-76      | 16,903 | 17,955  | 27,943  | .61  | .64 |
| Carter 1977-80    | 16,563 | 17,825  | 28,699  | .58  | .62 |
| Reagan 1981-84    | 15,099 | 16,710  | 26,989  | .56  | .62 |

[a]Income figures are averages over the indicated years.
Source: Data from *Economic Report of the President Transmitted to Congress,* Washington, DC: Government Printing Office.

White family incomes also fell under Reagan. White families' average median income of $26,989 was the second lowest since the 1967-68 Johnson years. Given their loyalties in the 1980 presidential election, it is ironic that their best income performance took place during the preceding Carter administration.

Undoubtedly one of the major reasons average black family income is as low as it is is because of the large and increasing proportion of black female-headed families, an issue we will return to below. Table 2-11 shows that in 1973, 34% of all black families were headed by a female, while nearly 62% were husband-wife. This compares to 10% white female-headed and nearly 88% white husband-wife families. By 1987 black female-headed families represented almost 43% of all black families and married couple families were down to 51%. White female-headed families had also risen by 1987 to about 13% and white married families had fallen somewhat to 83%.

Thus if, as in table 2-12, we consider only married-couple families, the black-white median family income ratios improve considerably in percentage terms, although the trend in the last eight or nine years has been quite flat.

One would expect black married-couple families to do better relative to white families than black families taken as a whole not only because of the presence of a high number of black female-headed families but also because of the high relative proportion of black working wives in black married-couple families.

As shown in table 2-13, in 1973 nearly 52% of the wives in black married-couple families worked compared to 41% of their white counterparts. By 1987 the proportion of black working wives had increased to 66% while that of white working wives had increased to 55%.

The relative penury of the black female-headed family is revealed in the differential between their incomes and those of white and black married couple families, as well as white female-headed families. With respect to the latter, in 1973 a black family headed by a female had only 64% as much income on average as a similar white family. By 1987 this was down to 57%. In 1973 a black female-headed family had only 32% as much income as a white married-couple family; by 1987 this was down to 28%. In both 1973 and 1984, a white female-headed family had about half as much income as a white married-couple family. Among blacks, in 1973, a black female-headed family had 44% as much income as a black married-couple family; by 1987 the proportion had fallen to 36%.

Thus, with nearly half of all black families headed by a female and with the average income of such families less than a third that available to white married-couple families, it is difficult to be upbeat about the economic condition of the black family, the most important center of black life.

While there is not a great deal of comparative data on family wealth and asset ownership, what little there is tells an even more dismal tale about the relative economic plight of black families than does the income comparison. Table 2-14 reproduces census data on net worth and asset ownership. According to the census study, net worth is defined as the value of interest-earning assets (such as savings accounts,

## Table 2-11

Distribution of Family, by Family Type, for Selected Years, 1973-1987

| Year | Total | Black Married Couple Family | White Married Couple Family | Black Female-Headed Family | White Female-Headed Family |
|---|---|---|---|---|---|
| 1973 | 100% | 61.8% | 87.7% | 34.0% | 9.9% |
| 1974 | 100 | 60.9 | 86.9 | 35.3 | 10.5 |
| 1975 | 100 | 60.0 | 86.8 | 35.9 | 10.8 |
| 1976 | 100 | 58.7 | 86.7 | 37.1 | 10.9 |
| 1977 | 100 | 56.1 | 85.9 | 39.2 | 11.5 |
| 1979 | 100 | 55.5 | 85.6 | 40.5 | 11.6 |
| 1980 | 100 | 53.7 | 85.1 | 41.7 | 11.9 |
| 1981 | 100 | 55.1 | 84.5 | 40.6 | 12.4 |
| 1983 | 100 | 51.6 | 84.4 | 43.1 | 12.6 |
| 1984 | 100 | 51.2 | 83.9 | 43.7 | 12.8 |
| 1985 | 100 | 53.2 | 83.5 | 41.5 | 12.9 |
| 1986 | 100 | 52.7 | 83.4 | 41.8 | 13.0 |
| 1987 | 100 | 51.3 | 83.2 | 42.8 | 12.9 |

Source: See table 2-2.

## Table 2-12

### Black-White Median Family Income Ratios, by Family Type, Selected Years, 1973-1987

| Year | Black-White Married Couple Income Ratio | Black-White Female Head Income Ratio | Black Female Head/White Married Couple Income Ratio | White Female Head/White Married Couple Income Ratio | Black Female Head/Black Married Couple Income Ratio |
|---|---|---|---|---|---|
| 1973[a] | .72 | .64 | .32 | .50 | .44 |
| 1974[a] | .74 | .61 | .32 | .52 | .43 |
| 1975[a] | .76 | .64 | .33 | .51 | .43 |
| 1976[a] | .78 | .62 | .31 | .50 | .39 |
| 1977[a] | .75 | .64 | .31 | .49 | .42 |
| 1979[a] | .77 | .60 | .32 | .53 | .41 |
| 1980[b] | .79 | .62 | .32 | .51 | .40 |
| 1981[b] | .77 | .60 | .30 | .49 | .38 |
| 1983[b] | .79 | .58 | .29 | .50 | .37 |
| 1984[b] | .78 | .57 | .29 | .50 | .37 |
| 1985[b] | .78 | .59 | .29 | .50 | .38 |
| 1986[b] | .80 | .59 | .28 | .47 | .35 |
| 1987[b] | .77 | .57 | .28 | .48 | .36 |

[a]Family heads 14 years and older
[b]Family heads 15 years and older
Source: See table 2-2.

## Table 2-13

Black-White Working Wives in Married-Couple Families,
by Percentage, Selected Years, 1973-1987

| Year | Black Wives in Labor Force | White Wives in Labor Force |
|------|---------------------------|----------------------------|
| 1973 | 51.5% | 40.7% |
| 1974 | 53.5 | 42.3 |
| 1975 | 56.8 | 43.0 |
| 1976 | 56.8 | 44.4 |
| 1977 | 58.0 | 45.2 |
| 1979 | 59.1 | 48.4 |
| 1980 | 59.6 | 49.3 |
| 1981 | 59.8 | 49.4 |
| 1983 | 63.3 | 51.3 |
| 1984 | 64.0 | 52.5 |
| 1985 | 64.1 | 52.9 |
| 1986 | 65.4 | 54.3 |
| 1987 | 65.8 | 55.3 |

Source: See table 2-2.

## Table 2-14

### Median Families Net Worth, 1984

| Net Worth by Income | Black | White | Black-White Ratio | White-Black Ratio |
|---|---|---|---|---|
| Median Net Worth (All Households) | $3,397 | $39,135 | .09 | 11.52 |
| Less than $10,800 | 88 | 8,443 | .01 | 95.94 |
| $10,800 to $23,999 | 4,218 | 30,514 | .14 | 7.28 |
| $24,000 to $45,999 | 15,977 | 50,529 | .32 | 3.16 |
| $48,000 plus | 58,758 | 128,237 | .46 | 2.18 |

### Median Net Worth, by Family Type, 1984

| Family Type | Black | White | Black-White Ratio | White-Black Ratio |
|---|---|---|---|---|
| Married-Couple Families | $13,061 | $54,184 | .24 | 4.15 |
| Female-Headed Families | 671 | 22,500 | .03 | 33.53 |

Source: U. S. Bureau of Census, *Current Population Reports*, Series P-70, No. 7, Household Wealth and Asset Ownership: 1984, Table G, p. 5.

money-market deposit accounts, certificates of deposit, interest-earning checking accounts, money-market funds, corporate and municipal bonds, U.S. government securities), stocks and mutual fund shares, residential and rental property, vacation homes and land holdings, a business or profession, mortgages held by sellers, and motor vehicles, less liabilities in the form of any debts secured by any asset, credit cards, store bills, bank loans, or other unsecured debts.

According to the data displayed in table 2-14, in 1984 the median net worth of a black family was approximately $3,400, while that of a white family was almost 12 times as much at approximately $39,000. Another way to look at it is that for every $1 in wealth held by a white family a comparable black family had 9 cents in wealth. For those families with incomes under $11,000 (the "official" poverty population), white families had 96 times greater net worth than blacks. White families with incomes between $11,000 and $48,000 (the broad middle class) had 3 to 7 times more wealth than their black counterparts. White families with incomes in excess of $48,000 had twice the wealth of blacks in that category.

The breakdown by family type shows that white married-couple families had four times more wealth than black married-couple families; and white female-headed families had nearly 34 times more wealth than black female-headed families. White female-headed families on average had greater net worth than black married couple families.

Blacks and whites also diverge when it comes to the composition of asset ownership. According to the census study, "Compared with White householders, Black householders held a greater percentage of their net worth in durable goods such as housing (65% versus 41%) and motor vehicles (11% versus 6%), and a lower percentage in financial assets such as stocks and mutual fund shares (1% versus 7%) and deposits at financial institutions (7% versus 15%)" (U.S. Bureau of the Census, 1983b).

Much is often made of the narrow gap in black and white female income and earnings as evidence for the healthy state of the black economy (see table 2-15). The black-white female median income ratios for year-round, full-time workers in all age groups increased over the 1967 to 1984 period. In 1967 a typical black female full-time worker had an income that was 75% of the income of a similarly placed white female. By 1984 her income was 90% as much. Indeed, in 1979, 20- to 24-year-old black women reached parity with white women. And although there was a general decline in the income ratios of younger women over the mid- to late-1970s, they are still in a better position vis-a-vis white women than black men are relative to white men.

However, in measuring the incomes of black women against those of white women one needs to deal with a much more significant background: the fact that both groups are at a disadvantage in the labor market, that both groups receive substandard incomes. Measuring the progress of one solely in terms of the other gives an incomplete and misleading picture of the economic conditions of each.

## Table 2-15

Black-White Female Median Income Ratios for Year-Round,
Full-Time Workers, by Age Cohorts, 1967-1984

| Year | All Ages[a] | 20-24 | 25-34 | 35-44 | 45-54 | 55-64 |
|------|-------------|-------|-------|-------|-------|-------|
| 1967 | .75 | .81 | .76 | .75 | .72 | .58 |
| 1968 | .76 | .83 | .79 | .76 | .74 | .61 |
| 1969 | .80 | .83 | .81 | .86 | .70 | .70 |
| 1970 | .82 | .93 | .87 | .86 | .71 | .60 |
| 1971 | .88 | .99 | .92 | .88 | .84 | .70 |
| 1972 | .86 | .95 | .86 | .83 | .82 | .72 |
| 1973 | .85 | .88 | .89 | .80 | .80 | .72 |
| 1974 | .91 | .96 | .94 | .89 | .83 | .79 |
| 1975 | .96 | .99 | .97 | .93 | .87 | .73 |
| 1976 | .94 | .99 | .93 | .93 | .87 | .75 |
| 1977 | .94 | .96 | .91 | .93 | .91 | .74 |
| 1978 | .93 | .96 | .92 | .88 | .97 | .77 |
| 1979 | .92 | 1.00 | .90 | .94 | .88 | .79 |
| 1980 | .93 | .95 | .93 | .90 | .94 | .84 |
| 1981 | .90 | .88 | .92 | .82 | .88 | .80 |
| 1982 | .89 | .92 | .94 | .88 | .82 | .77 |
| 1983 | .89 | .88 | .84 | .94 | .87 | .74 |
| 1984 | .90 | .89 | .86 | .97 | .90 | .86 |

[a]Includes persons 14 years and older in 1967-1978, and 15 years and older in 1979-1984
Source: See table 2-1.

A more instructive approach is that taken in table 2-16, where incomes of both black females and white females are compared with those of white males, the benchmark group. Median income ratios are presented both for all workers and year-round, full-time workers. Mean income ratios (such as those for males in table 2-6), corrected to include persons without income, are also shown. The latter ratios and those for all workers are quite similar.

While all three statistics show that both black- and white-female incomes relative to those of white males have been on the increase since 1967, they also show how low those relative incomes were and still are. Among all workers, a black female had an income that was only 25% that of a white male in 1967. This proportion steadily increased to 37% in 1984. If the black female was a year-round, full-time worker, her proportion went from 43% in 1967 to 57% in 1984. However, as table 2-4 indicates, only 32 to 35% of black-females in the labor force were year-round, full-time workers during the 1967-1984 period, and so they do not fully represent the economic reality of black-female workers. "All Workers and All Persons" categories are more relevant for the consideration of relative black-female incomes, categories hardly illustrative of black economic progress.

It is inappropriate to leave the problem of black relative incomes without at least a passing glance at one of the proximate sources of the problem: black relative unemployment. The black unemployment rate is twice that of the white rate, as we see in table 2-17. Whether the group observed is blacks alone or blacks and other races the "twice the white rate" results are generally the same. These results have ominous new implications when coupled with the research Bluestone and Harrison (1986) have done on the types of jobs available to blacks in the new economy. They found that, between 1973 and 1979, 29% of net new employment among nonwhite males occurred in "low" wage jobs (those that paid $7,000 or less in 1984 dollars). Between 1979 and 1984, nearly 65% of all net new employment among nonwhite males was in such jobs. At the same time, between 1973 and 1979, 42% of net new employment of nonwhite males was in "high" wage jobs (those that paid $28,000 or more in 1984 dollars). Between 1973 and 1979, net new employment among nonwhite females was about 5% in low wage jobs and 10% in high wage jobs. Between 1979 and 1984, net new employment in low wage jobs had increased to 34%, while that in high wage jobs had fallen to 4%.

These trends suggest that the prospects for the black unemployed are increasingly limited and limiting. Commenting on the results of their study, Bluestone and Harrison state:

> Employment for both minority men and minority women shows a renewed trend toward low wages. Notable in this regard is the apparent reversal of the trend toward higher wage job opportunities for black men which was observed during much of the 1970s. (1986)

## Table 2-16

Median and Mean Income Ratios for Black Females, White Females, and White Males, 1967-1984

| Year | All Worker Median Income | | | "Corrected" Mean Income | | | Full-Time Median Income | | |
|---|---|---|---|---|---|---|---|---|---|
| | Black Female/ White Male | White Female/ White Male | Black Female/ White Female | Black Female/ White Male | White Female/ White Male | Black Female/ White Female | Black Female/ White Male | White Female/ White Male | Black Female/ White Female |
| 1967 | .25 | .28 | .78 | .25 | .28 | .89 | .43 | .58 | .75 |
| 1968 | .26 | .33 | .79 | .25 | .28 | .91 | .44 | .58 | .76 |
| 1969 | .27 | .32 | .84 | .26 | .28 | .91 | .46 | .58 | .80 |
| 1970 | .29 | .32 | .91 | .27 | .29 | .95 | .48 | .59 | .82 |
| 1971 | .30 | .34 | .88 | .28 | .29 | .96 | .51 | .58 | .88 |
| 1972 | .31 | .33 | .93 | .28 | .29 | .98 | .48 | .57 | .86 |
| 1973 | .30 | .33 | .93 | .27 | .29 | .93 | .47 | .56 | .85 |
| 1974 | .32 | .36 | .90 | .29 | .31 | .94 | .51 | .56 | .91 |
| 1975 | .33 | .37 | .91 | .31 | .32 | .96 | .55 | .57 | .96 |
| 1976 | .34 | .36 | .94 | .32 | .33 | .96 | .55 | .59 | .94 |
| 1977 | .33 | .38 | .86 | .32 | .34 | .94 | .54 | .58 | .94 |
| 1978 | .32 | .36 | .92 | .33 | .36 | .91 | .55 | .59 | .93 |
| 1979 | .32 | .35 | .92 | .33 | .38 | .88 | .54 | .59 | .92 |
| 1980 | .34 | .37 | .93 | .34 | .40 | .86 | .55 | .59 | .93 |
| 1981 | .34 | .39 | .89 | .34 | .41 | .84 | .54 | .60 | .90 |
| 1982 | .36 | .40 | .88 | .36 | .43 | .83 | .56 | .62 | .89 |
| 1983 | .36 | .42 | .86 | .37 | .45 | .82 | .56 | .63 | .89 |
| 1984 | .37 | .42 | .89 | .38 | .45 | .84 | .57 | .63 | .90 |

Source: See table 2-2.

## Table 2-17

Black-White Unemployment Rates, Selected Years, 1948-1987

| Year | Black Males | White Males | Black-White Ratio | Black Females | White Females | Black-White Ratio |
|---|---|---|---|---|---|---|
| 1948[a] | 5.8 | 3.4 | 1.71 | 6.1 | 3.4 | 1.79 |
| 1953[a] | 4.8 | 2.5 | 1.92 | 4.1 | 3.1 | 1.32 |
| 1958[a] | 13.8 | 6.1 | 2.26 | 10.8 | 6.2 | 1.74 |
| 1963[a] | 20.5 | 4.7 | 2.23 | 11.2 | 5.8 | 1.93 |
| 1968[a] | 5.6 | 2.6 | 2.15 | 8.3 | 4.3 | 1.93 |
| 1973[a] | 7.7 | 3.8 | 2.03 | 10.6 | 5.3 | 2.00 |
| 1978[a] | 11.0 | 4.6 | 2.39 | 13.0 | 6.2 | 2.10 |
| 1983[b] | 20.3 | 8.8 | 2.31 | 18.6 | 7.9 | 2.35 |
| 1986[b] | 14.8 | 6.0 | 2.47 | 14.2 | 6.1 | 2.33 |
| 1987[b] | 12.7 | 5.4 | 2.35 | 13.2 | 5.2 | 2.54 |

[a]Blacks and other races
[b]Blacks alone
Sources: U.S. Dept. of Labor, *Manpower-Report to the President,* 1982, table A-28. Bureau of Labor Statistics, *Employment and Earnings Annual Averages,* January 1984 and January 1987.

The racial gap is palpable, and yet it is not closing. To gain a richer understanding of the causes and the characteristics of the gap requires a careful discussion of two central phenomena: (1) the transition, over the course of the twentieth century, from capitalism to the managerial estate and (2) evolving patterns of class differentiation throughout American society and, specifically, within the native black population. Not only can the gap be best understood in such a context, but the context will illuminate the failure of a variety of strategies developed to close the gap, as well as the likely failure of certain "new" strategies being developed today.

The discussion undertaken here will also demonstrate the paradox that confronts native blacks in pursuit of equality in a society infused with and characterized by inequality. In a society with as dense a hierarchical structure as that of the United States, racial equality, much like gender equality, depends upon and demands a fundamental alteration of the structure itself. The analysis set out here should pose clearly the issues at stake for the survival and salvation of black America.

Finally, it should be noted at the outset that the use of the term "native blacks" is intended to emphasize that this report refers only to the historic black population in the United States, whose cultural and genealogical origins can be traced to the age of plantation slavery in North America. The essay does not analyze the conditions of more recent black immigrants–such as those from the Caribbean, West Africa, Ethiopia, or Uganda. This exclusion is not because of insensitivity to nor lack of interest in their circumstances but because many aspects of their experiences are special to them and would require an entirely separate analysis.

The term "native blacks" is also used to avoid the ideologically popular term "minorities." The latter term has contributed to confounding the race question, which has stood at the heart of this nation's history since its founding, with a more recent panoply of "causes" that promote the interests of groups ranging from women to homosexuals to Vietnamese refugees. The idea of "minorities" deflects us from the main issue–the historical race question in the United States.

## The Black Family in the Managerial Age

The data already presented documents the lagging economic condition of the black family. But this condition is only one indicator of the scope of the crisis confronting America's native black population. To understand its full dimensions requires a substantive historical inquiry into the evolving scheme of social relations in contemporary America.

The two-parent family has long been the norm in American society. Among the various racial and ethnic subgroups in the United States, the native black population has experienced the most drastic decline in the representation of this traditional family structure. The fraction of black families headed by women has grown from 25% in the 1950s to 50% in recent years. It is among this growing group of black families headed by mothers that poverty strikes hardest and most harshly (Darity & Myers,

1984). Single-parent status also appears to be correlated with a variety of disadvantages for children that extend far beyond the direct limitations imposed by poverty status. For example, a child from a single-parent family has a greater probability of dropping out of school (Shaw, 1982; McLanahan, 1985). Although it is less well-documented, it has also been observed that juvenile delinquency and early pregnancies can be attributed to the experience of growing up in single-parent families.

The growth of female-headed families among blacks is symptomatic of conditions that lie well below the surface of statistics, well below such catch phrases as the "feminization of poverty." These phenomena are linked to the precarious status of black America as a whole in the current social milieu. The prevalence of black female-headed families is merely an indicator of an entire constellation of forces that negatively affect black Americans in our society.

The husband-wife family has always been relatively less the case among blacks than among other ethnic or racial groups in the United States. Slaveholders sought the breakup of family, tribe, and clan to individualize and subordinate the black population. Not until the mature period of slavery, when importation of Africans had all but ceased, did the slaveholders seek, in some cases, to promote more conventional family life amongst their slaves. The slaveholders' motives, of course, were commercial; they sought some measure of family stability to ensure a stable labor supply. The commercial value of the chattel was the dominant consideration, leading the slaveholders to buy and sell slaves without consideration for relational ties. From the outset, then, black family life was assaulted in America; indeed, such assault was both fundamental to and a function of the system.

Emancipation led to feverish attempts to bring family members together. However, many former slaves remained unattached to any family unit because no family members could be found. The post-Reconstruction period was also characterized by an attempt on the part of the white aristocracy to regain control over black labor. The mechanism that restored many of the features of slave labor was the prison-lease system. The prison-lease system contributed to the ongoing breakup of the black family by simultaneously removing married black males from their families and preventing unmarried black males from forming new families.

Largely confined to the unskilled categories of the national labor market, black male labor was still viewed as valuable, at least in a reserve capacity, by industrialists in the early twentieth century. Industrialists turned to black workers as strike-breakers and as a pool of available cheaper wage contestants in the labor market. The movement of black workers from the South to the urban North, in response to such calls for cheaper labor, led to additional familial dislocations.[4]

Thus the forces undermining the black family from slavery times through the early part of the present century were consequences of attempts to utilize and control black labor–particularly black male labor–both within the slave system and the system that evolved after slavery. But from the 1930s onward the forces undermining the black family increasingly have been associated with a perceived lack of necessity of black labor–especially black male labor.

Whereas the conditions undermining the black family in the period prior to 1930s were the character of capitalist development, largely within southern agriculture, since that time the conditions undermining the black family have been due to the development of a managerial society in the United States. Dominance by the business-financial elite in the United States gave way to dominance by the intellectuals and intelligentsia–the managerial class.[5]

The principle guiding capitalist development was the profitable command of labor, both labor in use and labor in reserve (unemployed); the principle guiding managerial development has been the scientific discharge of labor from the workplace, particularly manual labor. This pattern of discharge has meant the progressive marginalization of black males, long excluded from extensive participation in nonmanual and so-called "knowledge" occupations. Now large numbers of black males are faced with the elimination of the occupational categories for which they qualify. As the black male is moved further and further out to the margins of America's economy and society, this necessarily has repercussions for the black family.

The microelectronic-cum-robotics revolution has laid the groundwork for the elimination of a whole range of occupations, particularly manufacturing, without replacing those positions with new work. This is not a uniquely American phenomenon; it is occurring worldwide. A decade ago in a special report prepared for the president of France, Nora and Minic commented, "Given the increasing automation of industry, most industrial managers state that growth in the coming years will be accomplished without increases in manpower–in fact, that manpower will decrease slightly, unless demand rises at an unusual rate..." (1978, pp. 38-39). In a 1980 study prepared for the International Labour Office, Juan Rada concluded that "a transition is taking place from a society with unemployment to one that no longer needs its full potential labour force to produce the necessary goods and services under current conditions of work" (p. 105). In a similar vein, Ernest Mandel observed in his 1978 Marshall Lectures at Cambridge, "...new radical substitution of machines for men (in fact, the new wave of automation could be characterized as 'robotism') would almost unavoidably imply massive reduction in total productive employment" (1980, p. 108). Mandel specifically referred to studies in West Germany and Japan that revealed prospects for the massive elimination of industrial workers' jobs in both countries via robotics. In West Germany 4.3 workers per robot was the estimated reduction; in Japan estimates indicated that one-third of the existing industrial work force in 1978 could be eliminated by 1988, and 90% within 20 to 30 years, while maintaining 1978 levels of output.

In the United States, since late 1982 (as estimated by the Federal Reserve Board's index), manufacturing output has grown almost 30%, whereas employment in manufacturing grew only 6%. In 1986 output in manufacturing grew 1%, while the absolute number of jobs fell by 200,000. In the automobile industry the 1986 figures are even more striking. Wharton Econometrics estimates that output per hour has risen 5.6% while man-hours have fallen 3.2%. (Clark, 1986, p. 1). A study of these structural changes in the U.S. economy undertaken by Leontief and Duchin

(1986) leads them to conclude that the intensive use of automation will make it possible to achieve over the next 20 years significant economies in labor relative to the production of the same bills of goods with the technologies currently in use. And who is to say what the consequences of future technologies will be?

Charles Silberman (1966) issued an early challenge to this scenario in the 1960s. He suggested that despite his own expectation that eventually "we shall have the technical capability to substitute machines for men in most of the functions men now perform...the decision to automate would still be an investment decision–not a scientific decision." (p. 2). In effect he said that human labor can compete with machines by offering to work for lower wages: "In the last analysis, men will not be replaced by machines because widespread substitution of machines for men would tend to reduce the price of the latter and increase the price of the former..." (p. 22). This appears to be precisely the type of leverage exercised recently by Weyerhauser Corporation when it "weathered a six-week strike to force workers to accept wage cuts averaging 20%" (Clark, 1986 p. 20). Silberman's answer to those who contend that workers will be displaced relatively, and perhaps absolutely, by technical change is to point out that laborers can offer to work for less. Unless, however, the productivity gains lead to concomitant reductions in output prices, workers will be accepting real reductions in their standard of living.

What underlies Silberman's response is the belief that technical change will continue to be profit motivated. However, as capitalism winds down and the managerial era supplants it, "scientific decisions" are replacing "investment decisions." In such an environment, there will be no barrier to the replacement of labor with machinery. Devendra Garg (1986) estimates that the spread of automation throughout U.S. industry could have an effect on almost half of the work force; automation is unlikely to create as many jobs as it destroys because robots can build other robots.

Capitalist development originated the process of continuous, albeit unsteady, reductions in labor time. This reduction generated a reserve of labor, a reserve that is disproportionately black in the United States. This reserve–not employed but not unemployable–serves at least two functions: it provides employers with a ready pool of workers to draw upon during periods of rapid industrial expansion; and it serves as a restraint on the demands of employed workers (Marx, 1977).

In contrast, for the managerial class this reserve of labor is without function. As the momentum of technical change renders labor superfluous, from a managerial perspective the "excess" population carried over from capitalist to postcapitalist society is genuinely unnecessary (Darity, 1983). In a remarkably prescient study, Donald Michael (1962) identified a number of procedures to cope with a population that is not needed to perform work: (1) put people into public works projects, (2) relocate people to regions or nations where automation is not yet so extensive, (3) reduce the birth rate, and (4) lower the retirement age. Aside from procedure number three, Michael saw problems arising from each of these steps. He did not articulate the two gruesome alternatives of incarceration and extermination, but he was explicitly aware that when cybernation takes hold there will indeed be a population deemed extraneous and thus subject to containment measures.

The position of the black male–and the black population in general–must be understood in the context of these broader trends and developments. Black males are overwhelmingly members of the working class, and in particular are represented in the inactive or surplus portion of the working class. Among their numbers are a large percentage of persons rarely employed, deeply entrenched in poverty, most likely to be imprisoned, most likely to be the military's foot soldiers, and least likely to have a sense of optimism about the opportunities offered by American society. This segment of the black working class is referred to by sociologists as the black "underclass." (Wilson, 1980). Moreover, there is no evident place for them in the managerial age, as race and class harden into caste under circumstances where intergenerational social mobility becomes ever more elusive.

## Intraracial Inequality in the Managerial Age

The broad lines of class division that exist in America as a whole–between capital, labor, and the managerial class–are replicated in native black America. The black middle class consists of an intellectual-professional element as well as a business element. The latter element is of far less importance than the former, but the two combined comprise "the black elite."

The black business element is notorious for the relative modesty of its enterprises, as well as for the insignificance of its output in the U.S. economy as a whole. Romantic notions of "black capitalism" notwithstanding, the black business-person has never been a serious force, has never produced substantial economic progress in black America. When E. Franklin Frazier (1957) wrote his classic study of the black middle class he referred accurately to "the myths of Negro business." Those myths are still promulgated by some who fantasize about a black American entrepreneurial heyday, despite the marginal position of black business and the waning of the business age.[6] The black businessperson's wealth may be large relative to other blacks, but it is small relative to the wealth of white owners and directors of the nation's major corporations.

The second major element of the black elite is the intellectual-professional group–doctors, lawyers, ministers, educators, social workers, etc. This is the managerial strata of the black community. Its functional role has largely been the supervision and social management of the black working class.[7] It is this class that is the source of the ideological stance attributed to black America in general by the media, deeply attached to the idea of achieving racial equality. And it is useful to note, as Frazier observed, that "...from the beginning the Negro intelligentsia, or what Du Bois called the 'Talented Tenth,' was created by philanthropic foundations supported by northern industrialists"[8] (1957).

There is some ambiguity concerning the size of the black middle class. Those who identify it strictly in economic terms—for example, by characterizing as middle class all families of four with $20,000 or more in income in 1980 dollars—find that about 20% the black population is now middle class (McGhee, 1982). But the approach of this report is to identify class position by social function rather than merely by income. Educational credentials separate the black managerial class from the black working class in the same manner that educational credentials separate the managerial class in general from the masses.

Based upon this approach the black middle class may be only 7 to 10% of the black population. The precise number is not what really matters. What counts is that the black managerial class—despite substantial growth in the 1960s—is small in proportion to the overall black population, and especially small when compared with representation in the same class by the nonblack majority or by other ethnic groups in the United States.[9]

There is sharp divergence between the lifestyles, attitudes, perceptions, and material well-being of the members of the black managerial class and the black underclass. It is as if they are planets spinning on opposite sides of the sun. But at the same time that their contrasting experiences push these two elements of the black community further and further apart, the structure of post-New Deal social programs joins them at the hip, Siamese twins of welfare.

The gap between the black managerial class and the black underclass has statistical manifestations nearly as pronounced as the gap between blacks as a whole and the nonblack majority. The depths of the difference crystallize in the following observations:

- The black underclass is the site of the most fragile family circumstances. By 1981, 46%—almost half—of the approximately 6.4 million black families in the United States were headed by women (U.S. Bureau of Census, 1983b, p.102). These families with absent fathers form the heart of the black underclass. In 1981, 68% of such families with children under 18 years of age received incomes below the poverty line (U.S. Bureau of Census, 1983a, p. 8). The experiences of these women heading families contrast sharply with those of the black professional women who have children late in life or have none at all. But both groups face declining prospects for black male mates—black poor women because of the low relative numbers of marriageable black men and black professional women because of the low relative numbers of comparably educated black men. To point up this latter discrepancy, black women are now enrolling at major universities at two times the rate of black men.

- Court decisions related to family life have progressively pushed female-headed families toward reliance on social transfer programs as a means of support.[10] Today the welfare crisis can be identified justifiably with the crisis in black family life. Economist Richard Coe (1982), using longitudinal data from the University of Michigan's Panel Study of Income Dynamics, found that more than half of the recipients of welfare for eight or more years between 1969 and 1978 were black. In addition Coe found that nearly 60% of all black females who were heads of households or wives in 1970 received welfare at some point between 1969 and 1978. Among these women, 40% received welfare for five years or more, and 30% received welfare for eight years or more. (Also see tables 2-18 and 2-19.)

- In a broader sense, the black underclass is heavily dependent on federal transfer programs as a source of income. A 1983 report in *The Washington Post* revealed:

> One out of every four blacks in America is now enrolled in Medicaid, the largest federal welfare program. One in four gets food stamps, the second largest program. One out of every five receives aid to families with dependent children (AFDC), the largest welfare program that pays cash. One of every seven lives in federally subsidized housing. (Coleman, p. A1)

It is also pertinent to note here that while 2% of white male-headed families, 6% of black male-headed families, and 15% of white female-headed families received public assistance and welfare income in 1981, 40% of black female-headed families received those categories of income (see table 2-20). The mean dollar amount from these types of income received by black female-headed families came to more than $3,100 during the same year (p. 104).

It is easy to document black underclass dependence on the social programs inaugurated in the 1930s and greatly expanded in the 1960s. It is also easy to document, but less widely recognized, that the black managerial class is heavily dependent on these same programs from the other side of the fence: the earnings of black managerial class are received in large measure from public sector positions that involve administration of the social programs. The recent growth and "progress" of the black managerial class can be traced directly to the expansion of social welfare programs under the rubric of the Great Society. The following lengthy observation from Brown and Erie (1981) is especially pertinent:

> ... expanding public social welfare employment has served as a major port of entry for the new black middle class ... 55% of the 1960-76 increase in black professional, managerial, and technical employment (PATs) occurred in the public sector, compared with 34% for whites. Social welfare programs accounted for nearly one-half of the black middle-class increase, compared with one-quarter for whites. As of 1976, 45% of all black professionals, administrators, and technicians were in public social welfare programs, compared with 19% of

## Table 2-18

Welfare Recipients, by Length of Welfare Receipt, 1969-1978

| Number of Years of Welfare Receipt | Black | Total Population |
|---|---|---|
| 1 | 14.9[a] | 31.3 |
| 2-5 | 39.0 | 42.9 |
| 6-9 | 30.9 | 17.9 |
| 10 | 15.2 | 7.9 |

[a]14.9% of black persons who received welfare incomes at any time between 1969 and 1978 received it for only year.

Source: A Preliminary Empirical Examination of the Dynamics of Welfare Use, (p. 131), by R.D. Coe, in *Analysis of the First Twelve Years of the Panel Study of Income Dynamics,* Vol. 9 of *Five Thousand American Families– Patterns of Economic Progress,* 1974-, University of Michigan: Survey Research Center, Institute for Social Research.

## Table 2-19

Distribution of Population, by Number of Years of Welfare Receipt, 1969-1979

| Number of Years | Welfare[a] Receipt | | | Welfare Amounted to at Half of Income | | |
|---|---|---|---|---|---|---|
| | Black | White | Black as a Percent of Total | Black | White | Black as a Percent of Total |
| 0 | 51.0[b] | 83.9 | 6.0[c] | 66.1 | 91.3 | 8.3 |
| 1 | 7.9 | 4.9 | 13.7 | 6.6 | 1.9 | 40.6 |
| 2-5 | 20.8 | 6.6 | 26.3 | 14.3 | 4.1 | 41.4 |
| 6-9 | 14.2 | 3.2 | 49.6 | 9.8 | 2.0 | 56.9 |
| 10 | 6.2 | 1.4 | 54.8 | 3.2 | 0.7 | 55.3 |
| 1-10 | 49.0 | 16.1 | | 33.9 | 8.7 | |

[a]AFDC, SSI, general assistance payments, old age assistance, aid to the disabled, and food stamps.
[b]51% of the black population did not receive income from welfare in any year between 1969 and 1978.
[c]6% of the families who did not receive income from welfare in any year between 1969 and 1978 were black.
Source: See table 2-19, pp. 142, 163-164.

## Table 2-20

Families, by Race and Gender, of HEA with Income from
Public Assistance and Supplement Security Income, 1975-1983
(Percentage of Distribution)

| Year | Public Assistance & Supplemental Security Income | | | | Public Assist & Welfare Income | | | | Supplemental Security Income | | | |
|---|---|---|---|---|---|---|---|---|---|---|---|---|
| | Female | | Male | | Female | | Male | | Female | | Male | |
| | Black | White | Black | White | Black | White | Black | White | Black | White | Black | White |
| 1983 | 43.2a | 17.3 | 10.1 | 3.1 | 37.4 | 13.7 | 5.4 | 1.7 | 9.0 | 4.3 | 5.8 | 1.5 |
| 1982 | 42.2 | 18.2 | 10.4 | 2.0 | 37.2 | 14.6 | 6.1 | 1.7 | 8.0 | 4.5 | 5.0 | 1.4 |
| 1981 | 46.6 | 18.9 | 11.2 | 3.1 | 39.6 | 15.5 | 6.4 | 1.7 | 10.2 | 4.4 | 5.8 | 1.5 |
| 1980 | 46.2 | 19.4 | 12.1 | 3.2 | 38.2 | 15.9 | 7.4 | 1.9 | 12.0 | 4.9 | 5.7 | 1.5 |
| 1979 | 49.2 | 19.1 | 11.6 | 3.0 | 41.3 | 15.3 | 7.0 | 1.7 | 12.0 | 4.9 | 5.8 | 1.5 |
| 1978 | 55.0 | 24.4 | 13.0 | 3.2 | 46.5 | 19.8 | 7.8 | 1.8 | 11.5 | 6.0 | 6.2 | 1.6 |
| 1977 | 53.6 | 23.9 | 13.0 | 3.4 | 46.5 | 19.6 | 7.3 | 1.9 | 10.3 | 5.6 | 7.0 | 1.7 |
| 1976 | 55.0 | 24.9 | 12.3 | 3.4 | 48.6 | 20.3 | 7.5 | 1.9 | 11.0 | 5.9 | 6.0 | 1.7 |
| 1975 | 53.7 | 25.9 | 11.9 | 3.4 | 47.1 | 21.2 | 7.4 | 1.9 | 11.2 | 5.8 | 6.9 | 1.8 |

aIn 1983, 43.2% of black families with females heads received income from public assistance or supplemental security income at some time during that year.

Source: U.S. Bureau of Census, *Current Population Reports, Consumer Income,* No. 80, pp. 86, 88; No. 85, pp. 96, 98; No. 90, pp. 105, 107; No. 97, pp. 103, 105; No. 105, p. 126; No. 114, p. 127; No. 118, p. 119; No. 123, p. 148; No. 129, p. 138; No. 132, p. 116; No. 137, p. 104; No. 142, p. 104; No. 146, p. 105.

comparably situated whites. At the federal level, 42% of all black PATs were in DHEW, HUD, Labor, CSA, or the VA compared with 18% of whites. At the state and local level, 68% of all black PATs employed outside education (compared with 39% of whites) were in social welfare agencies. It is true that at least since the New Deal black professionals and administrators have been more likely to be employed in the public sector than whites. In this regard developments in the 1960s represent merely the extension of an historical trend. But if the attractiveness of public employment among the black middle class has not changed, something else has. Prior to 1960 black professionals and administrators were concentrated in education and, at the federal level, in the post office. The significant shift in the 1960s is that middle class blacks moved into noneducational social welfare agencies at the state and local level. Moreover, prior to 1960 the black middle class was relatively small. Between 1960 and 1976, the size of the black middle class roughly tripled. (pp. 308-309)

Herein lies the source of Richard Freeman's "dramatic progress" for blacks. The expansion of means-tested income maintenance programs for the poor under the aegis of the Great Society constituted an income maintenance program for the black managerial class as well. Tables 2-21 and 2-22 make clear the connection between growth in the black professional strata and social welfare employment. As Brown and Erie (1981) conclude:

The principal economic legacy of the Great Society for the black community...has been the creation of a large-scale social welfare economy of publicly funded middle-income service providers and low-income service and cash transfer receipts. (p. 311)

Here we find precisely how these two classes within black America are joined, while their daily lives gravitate in opposing directions.

The Great Society can thus be seen as a set of policy initiatives which, much like the New Deal, benefited the managerial class broadly. The specific impact on the black middle class was quite dramatic and points to a host of disturbing implications, the first of which concerns the black middle class's dream of racial equality. To the extent that racial inequality amounts to the black middle class being too small in number relative to the nonblack majority middle class, the obvious prescription is to expand further the black middle class. But if the expansion is conducted on the basis of increasing social welfare employment there must be clients to be served. Therefore, the black middle class, as constituted at present, needs a black underclass to justify its own occupational status. Too much racial equality undermines the service providers own reason for being. On the other hand, the alternative reform offered by the business interests—abolition of the welfare state—threatens to leave only the "private charities" to assist the poor, while other options offered by social managers, e.g.,

## Table 2-21[a]
### Social Welfare Employment Gains, by Gender and Race, 1960-1980

| | Nonagricultural Civilian Employment (in thousands)[b] | | | | | | | |
|---|---|---|---|---|---|---|---|---|
| | Females | | | | Males | | | |
| | White | | Black | | White | | Black | |
| Year | % | (N) | % | (N) | % | (N) | % | (N) |
| **1960** | | | | | | | | |
| Social Welfare[c] | 23.5% | | 20.0% | | 5.9% | | 8.5% | |
| Other | 76.5 | | 80.0 | | 94.1 | | 91.5 | |
| Total | 100.0 | (16269) | 100.0 | (2119) | 100.0 | (30706) | 100.0 | (2851) |
| **1969** | | | | | | | | |
| Social Welfare | 26.7 | | 29.3 | | 8.6 | | 10.9 | |
| Other | 73.3 | | 70.7 | | 91.4 | | 89.1 | |
| Total | 100.0 | (23363) | 100.0 | (3122) | 100.0 | (37326) | 100.0 | (3842) |
| **1973** | | | | | | | | |
| Social Welfare | 29.1 | | 34.8 | | 9.2 | | 12.5 | |
| Other | 70.9 | | 65.2 | | 90.8 | | 87.5 | |
| Total | 100.0 | (26202) | 100.0 | (3147) | 100.0 | (40012) | 100.0 | (4072) |
| **1977** | | | | | | | | |
| Social Welfare | 30.2 | | 35.8 | | 10.4 | | 11.9 | |
| Other | 69.8 | | 64.2 | | 89.6 | | 88.1 | |
| Total | 100.0 | (29651) | 100.0 | (3674) | 100.0 | (41213) | 100.0 | (3994) |
| **1980** | | | | | | | | |
| Social Welfare | 30.2 | | 39.0 | | 10.6 | | 13.4 | |
| Other | 69.8 | | 61.0 | | 89.4 | | 86.6 | |
| Total | 100.0 | (33428) | 100.0 | (4168) | 100.0 | (43362) | 100.0 | (4224) |
| **Social Welfare Share of Employment Increase** | | | | | | | | |
| 1960-1980 | 36.5% | | 58.6% | | 22.0% | | 23.6% | |
| 1960-1969 | 34.3 | | 49.1 | | 21.2 | | 18.0 | |
| 1969-1973 | 48.9 | | 92.9 | | 17.0 | | 38.7 | |
| 1973-1977 | 38.6 | | 49.0 | | 50.4 | | (43.6)[d] | |
| 1977-1980 | 30.2 | | 37.0 | | 14.4 | | 39.6 | |

[a]Table provided by M.K. Brown.
[b]As reported in March survey week.
[c]Includes medical, hospital, education, welfare, and religious employment.
[d]Social welfare share of employment decrease for black males, 1973-1977.
Sources: U.S. Bureau of the Census, *Public Use Sample*, 1960; U.S. Bureau of the Census, *Current Population Survey*, 1969, 1973, 1977, and 1980, March Supplement. Data tapes supplied by the Inter-University Consortium for Political Research, University of Michigan.

## Table 2-22[a]

Professional, Administrative and Technical Employment Gains, by Gender and Race, 1960-1980[b]

| | Nonagricultural Civilian Employment (in thousands)[b] | | | | | | | |
|---|---|---|---|---|---|---|---|---|
| | Females | | | | Males | | | |
| | White | | Black | | White | | Black | |
| Year | % | (N) | % | (N) | % | (N) | % | (N) |
| 1960 | | | | | | | | |
|   Social Welfare[c] | | | | | | | | |
|   Other | 24.3 | | 9.7 | | 81.9 | | 40.6 | |
|   Total | 100.0 | (2911) | 100.0 | (185) | 100.0 | (6436) | 100.0 | (138) |
| 1973 | | | | | | | | |
|   Social Welfare | 69.6 | | 81.8 | | 22.3 | | 44.9 | |
|   Other | 30.4 | | 18.2 | | 77.7 | | 55.1 | |
|   Total | 100.0 | (5220) | 100.0 | (488) | 100.0 | (11024) | 100.0 | (401) |
| 1977 | | | | | | | | |
|   Social Welfare | 65.8 | | 80.8 | | 23.8 | | 38.6 | |
|   Other | 34.2 | | 19.2 | | 76.2 | | 61.4 | |
|   Total | 100.0 | (6460) | 100.0 | (614) | 100.0 | (12271) | 100.0 | (479) |
| 1980 | | | | | | | | |
|   Social Welfare | 61.0 | | 77.7 | | 22.8 | | 35.9 | |
|   Other | 39.0 | | 22.3 | | 77.2 | | 64.1 | |
|   Total | 100.0 | (8281) | 100.0 | (670) | 100.0 | (13518) | 100.0 | (530) |
| Social Welfare Share of PAT Employment Increase | | | | | | | | |
|   1960-1980 | 53.0% | | 72.8% | | 27.1% | | 27.6% | |
|   1960-1973 | 61.9 | | 76.6 | | 28.2 | | 37.3 | |
|   1973-1977 | 49.8 | | 77.0 | | 37.0 | | 6.4 | |
|   1977-1980 | 43.9 | | 44.6 | | 13.0 | | 9.8 | |

[a]Table provided by M.K. Brown.
[b]As reported in March survey week.
[c]Includes medical, hospital, education, welfare, and religious employment.
Sources: See table 2-2.

Senator Moynihan's recent enthusiasm for workfare arrangements, are unremittingly punitive in character.

The second related implication of the policies of the Great Society concerns the tendency of the black managerial class–like the managerial class broadly–to support programmatic initiatives alleged to uplift all blacks when, in fact, the managers are the main beneficiaries. If the entire nexus of policies adopted in the 1960s are taken as a whole, not one can be found to have a net positive impact on the condition of the black underclass. For instance, Charles Brown has found that if affirmative action has had an effect on behalf of blacks, the effect appears to be concentrated among blacks "at the upper end of the skill distribution" (1982, p.60). Balancing and busing to achieve school desegregation left unaddressed the more fundamental issue of quality education. Antidiscrimination laws for housing were largely irrelevant for those financially unable to buy a new home. Manpower training programs prepared participants for nonexistent or marginal jobs. As pointed out above, the general expansion of transfer programs has reinforced the dependent status of the black underclass–dependent on federal largesse–and it has also nurtured the growth of the black managerial class. This is not to say that the Civil Rights Act of 1964 should not have been passed. It is to say that it did not and could not address the fundamental sources of racial inequality.

The peculiar vulnerability of the black middle class now becomes clear in the context of the greater class war. The Reagan administration's budget cutbacks–especially those aimed at social welfare programs–amounted to a direct assault on the occupations obtained by members of the black elite during the recent period of "dramatic progress." With the Reagan retrenchment well underway the consequences were already being felt. As *The Washington Post* reported in 1983:

> At the federal level, blacks and members of other minority groups accounted for one of every three persons laid off or downgraded as a result of Reagan retrenchment. Black administrators were laid off at a rate three times that of white administrators and nearly three and one-half times that of lower-level black employees. (Coleman, p. A18)

Still, the impact has not yet been as devastating as one might have expected because Congress stabilized expenditures and state and local governments took on a greater role in maintaining social welfare programs. Nevertheless, the peculiar vulnerability of the black middle class has been clearly exposed.

It is no surprise, then, that the black middle class stood in opposition to the Reagan agenda. Their tendency, however, was to revert back to endorsement of the social programs that gave them their moment in the sun, despite those programs' failure to uplift the black masses. The reversion carries some still deeper dangers.

Corporate capital's mission, which found its strategic expression in Reagan policies, is to curb the pretensions of the managerial class–to make some members of that class efficient functionaries on behalf of business and to cast others back into the working class where they may be made over into productive laborers.

On the other hand, the managerial class, particularly the broader nonblack element, will find less and less reason to retain the excess population. Its rational view of production–unmotivated by the pursuit of profit–leads it to see no compelling reason to maintain a reserve of unemployed workers. Over the long term it will move to eliminate superfluous layers of the working class. Since those layers most likely to be deemed superfluous are disproportionately black (as Wilhelm anticipated in *Who Needs the Negro?*), these are grim times indeed for the black underclass. Moreover, as the black underclass is reduced, the segment of the black population that "ministers" to the underclass–the black managerial class–also will have no social function. What purpose is there for service providers if there are no service recipients?

The superfluity of the black underclass is reinforced by technological developments (microelectronics-cum-robotics) that reduce the social necessity for all labor. It is aggravated further by the new immigrants who stand as replacements–for the new immigrants are less jaded, less rebellious, and less expensive workers.

In the short term the broad managerial class may promise *and deliver* a renewed expansion of social programs to garner the political support of both the black managerial class and the black underclass. But the longer term tendency is for the broad managerial class to prune away superfluous elements. Once power is consolidated the voting support of black Americans will no longer be required and the cost of maintenance of the disruptive and nonaccommodative black poor will come to be viewed as too expensive. Steps will be taken to prune away the black underclass, and, concomitantly, the black social managers as well.

While capitalist society sought to make every black a laborer, managerial society calls into question the utility of blacks. Managerial society is in the process of declaring "the Negro" obsolete. Capitalist society threatened the class status of the black elite, but the managerial revolution threatens the very existence of black America as a cultural entity.

This threat is implicit in the silence of the new managerial strategy on the race question. The New Industrial Policy (NIP), the economic prong of the "new" ideas being advanced by the managerial class, amounts to nothing more than a "trickle down" argument concerning benefits for black America.[11] Only now the "trickle down" benefits would emanate from a recovery engineered through national planning rather than a recovery engineered, as Reaganomics would have it, through the "natural" workings of the "free" market. On the rare occasions when proponents of NIP advance specific solutions to improve the black condition, they merely echo the New Deal-Civil Rights-Great Society programs.

Suffice it to say, *neither* path offers an authentic beacon of hope for the black underclass, nor for the black population at large. Ralph Bunche (1936), when confronted with a similar unsatisfactory fork in the road in the 1930s, reached a similar conclusion:

> For the Negro population, the New Deal means the same thing, but more of it. Striking at no fundamental social conditions, the New Deal at best can only fix the disadvantages, the differentials, the discriminations under which the Negro population has labored all along....
>
> ...New Deal planning only serves to crystallize those abuses and oppressions which the exploited Negro citizenry of America have long suffered under laissez-faire capitalism, and for the same reasons as in the past. (pp. 62, 65)

The choice now appears to be between a refurbished laissez-faire capitalism and a new New Deal. Neither alternative holds much promise for closing the gap for black America. Both alternatives contain threats to the survival and salvation of native black America.

## Discrimination in the Managerial Age

As the necessity for labor in the aggregate–particularly unskilled or low-skilled labor–continues to decline, the struggle to secure the remaining places on the occupational ladder will intensify. Racial and ethnic conflict will continue apace as groups seek to secure niches in the hierarchy of managerial society. In such an environment racial discrimination will continue, transmuted along new and more subtle lines by antidiscrimination legislation and litigation.

The dimensions of discrimination by race are vast, ranging from the exclusion of black youths from college preparatory tracks, to channelling black youths away from hard sciences, to outright exclusion from occupations. Particularly striking is the changing character of exclusion following the introduction of federal antidiscrimination measures. These measures did not address the power base of other ethnic contestants for occupational turf nor the incentives that exist for turf preservation. Only the decorative exteriors of discrimination were addressed, not the brick and mortar. The laws have merely produced new procedures to perpetuate exclusion. In their recent study on the structure of earnings, Taylor, Gwartney-Gibbs, and Farley (1986) find no sector of the U.S. economy that does not display significant discriminatory earnings differentials in the aftermath of antidiscrimination legislation.

In many different occupations, including jobs in the public sector such as in police and fire departments, the ascent of white workers up the seniority ladder was made easier because nonwhites were systematically excluded from competition for these jobs. Various union seniority systems were established at a time when racial minorities were barred from employment and union membership. Obviously blacks as a group, not just as individuals, constituted a class of victims who could not develop seniority status. A seniority system launched under these conditions inevitably becomes the institutionalized mechanism whereby whites as a group are granted racial privilege.[12]

But in the unfolding managerial age it is neccessary to look out for mechanisms and sites of exclusion other than those traditionally associated with union activity. In the age of science and technology it is the academy that assigns credibility, credentials, and the imprimatur of authority. How do native blacks fare in obtaining access to quality institutions of higher education?

One could just as well ask how blacks fare in obtaining quality educational experiences at all levels. The example of the city of Chicago is revealing. Nearly one-half of the students from Chicago's public schools do not finish high school, and this proportion is overwhelmingly black.[13] Of course without a high school diploma a student is not even eligible for college admission.

The University of Illinois at Chicago (UIC), which enrolls primarily a regional undergraduate student body, has undergone an overall enrollment decline since 1979. But the decline in black student enrollment has been 40%, considerably more significant than the overall drop. Moreover, among black students actually matriculating, the attrition rate is astonishing. Whereas 30.4% of white students entering UIC in the fall of 1981 had graduated by 1987, only 7.4% of the black students had. For the class entering in 1982, while 25% of the white students had graduated by 1987, only 4.4% of the black students had done so.[14]

The UIC case may be somewhat extreme but it is symptomatic of a national trend. At a major southern university, the University of North Carolina at Chapel Hill, black undergraduates experience academic suspension rates three times as high as those of white students.[15] The limited capacity of native blacks to gain from the academy and to influence the academy also is demonstrated by the drop in black enrollment in graduate schools. After peaking in the 1970s, the percentage of black graduate students has fallen from 5.1% in 1976 to 4.2% in 1982. Blacks remain a stable 4.6% of the professional school population. Sociologist Gail Thomas has offered the following explanations:

- The low quality of elementary and secondary schools in predominantly black areas channels black youths away from access to and interest in higher education.

- Guidance counselors fail to encourage black youths to pursue advanced degrees.

- The screening methods used to select students, given the traditionally poor performance of blacks on the SAT and the GRE, work against blacks whose performance on such tests is hampered by test bias and the lack of early and adequate exposure to standardized tests.

Consistent with the broader themes of this report Thomas warns, "Blacks are at a dangerous point in terms of becoming disempowered as a result of what I see as a disturbing trend in higher education..." (Associated Press, 1987, p. 17A).[16]

Blacks also are disappearing from the ranks of Ph.D.-holders. Fields such as engineering, the physical sciences, and mathematics now consistently have less than 2% black representation among their doctorates. Between 1977 and 1987 the number of doctorates awarded to black American males declined by 54% from 684 to 317, lower than the absolute number awarded to Asian-American men in the same year.[17] The cumulative effect of negligible black representation in these fields is a complete dearth of black influence in the dissemination of knowledge, credentials, status, and authority. It reinforces the marginal status of the native black population in the era of science and technology.

Again with respect to the specific Chicago case, across all Chicago area universities less than 3% of the faculties are black. Blacks are disproportionately untenured. It has been suggested that the lower tenure ratios for blacks are due to age (blacks on average are younger Ph.D. recipients) and due to the greater difficulty in obtaining tenure today. But the gap would persist even if the age distribution was the same, and even if tenure criteria had not stiffened, because a greater percent of blacks are on nontenure track appointments. For example, at UIC 32.7% of black and Hispanic faculty are not on tenure track compared with 17% of whites (Reis, 1987).

Further difficulties involve the concentration of black academics in history, sociology, and Afro-American studies. Moreover, less credibility is accorded research by black scholars doing racial research than is accorded white scholars. Black administrators, to a disproportionate degree, are not faculty members, making them more vulnerable to job loss if they take strong stands and less able to protect black faculty members faced with tenure denial. The fewer the blacks, the more prestigious the university. For example, in Chicago, while 14.9% of the faculty at Northeastern Illinois is black, only 2.6% of the faculty at Northwestern University is black (Reis, 1987).

The current trends seem locked in place, for the near term at least. Nationally in 1980-81 blacks received only 3.3% of undergraduate engineering degrees and a mere 1.6% of master's degrees. Less than 1% of engineering Ph.D.s were blacks. In 1980-81 blacks received 5.2% of the undergraduate degrees in biological sciences, largely from predominantly black schools, but only 2.9% of the master's degrees, and 1.7% of the Ph.D.s; blacks received 4% of the B.A.s in the physical sciences (also largely from black schools), 2% of the master's degrees, and 1% of the doctorates; and in mathematics, blacks received 5.3% the B.A.s (again largely from black schools), 2.6% of the master's degrees, and only 1.2% of Ph.D.s (Reis, 1987).

The American Council on Education estimates that American colleges and universities have 18,827 full-time black faculty–4% of the total, a drop from 19,674 in 1977. Blacks constitute only 2.3% of the faculty at predominantly white institutions; 8,200 black educators are concentrated at 100 predominantly black college campuses–institutions with less resources, less prestige, and less influence than their white counterparts (Duvall, 1987).

The phenomenon of black exclusion from the academy is of special significance in the managerial age. It indicates how widely the social dimensions of discriminatory practices stretch. The relative absence of blacks from the academy begins with the differential in opportunities afforded by family resources and the differential in the quality of schooling in the early years; it continues with the deflecting of black college students from fields with greater technical requirements; and it concludes with the ghettoization of the residual of black academics in a handful of less-respected subfields of research. Ultimately, blacks have negligible influence on the standards and procedures that govern access to the academy.

Antidiscrimination laws have not and cannot exercise much effect on these circumstances. Competition between ethnic and racial cliques produces the perpetuation of discrimination rather than its elimination. We are witnessing the historical outcome for the group that was always viewed by other (European) contesting groups as unworthy of entry into the ethnic social compromise over the allocation of occupational turf. Black workers consistently would be relegated to less-skilled jobs or denied jobs altogether. Matters only become worse when the range of available well-paid, blue-collar occupations narrow with structural change in the U.S. economy; after all, the discriminatory nature of the educational process inherently limits opportunities available to blacks.

## Conclusions

Race continues to matter. Discrimination persists, although its forms have altered. The intrinsic nature of American society is geared toward ethnic/racial competition, the struggle to carve out social turf for one's own group. The conflict works itself out in classic forms of American tribalism.

Blacks enter the turf wars with various disadvantages. Per capita income and (especially) wealth are comparatively low. Professional-level blacks frequently have supervisory or quasi-supervisory positions in social welfare administration, so that there is no significant basis for blacks to act independently of public sector "helping" positions. The relative deterioration of schooling, family life, health conditions, etc., all reinforce the disadvantages in racial/ethnic competition. And blacks have already lost many previous rounds of turf wars, since other contesting groups could all agree not to compromise with blacks. Class cleavages among blacks compound the difficulties in becoming successful competitors.

Familial and schooling crises are not uniquely black problems. These same symptoms of deterioration now appear among other groups. But among blacks these conditions are more acute and more visible, both anecdotally and statistically. And they layer on top of the inferior black position in America's ethnic/racial struggles.

If blacks are to be a healthy and contributing presence in the United States, the options are straightforward. Either the compromise must finally be struck, formally or informally, and native blacks granted an appropriate set of positions in managerial society's social structure, or a struggle must be waged against the structure itself. The former route means blacks must opt fully for a representative share of real (rather than merely racial) equality. The latter route means a far more radical course of action and would require calling into question the values that produced success in our competitive and hierarchical society.

I have touched upon the most troubling prospect of all: that a continued black presence is by no means assured. For in the transition from capitalism to managerialism those relegated to the surplus population will find their very existence threatened. In fact, to the extent that *blacks* are viewed as the social problem, and hence objects of social management, rather than the *system* being viewed as the social problem, the danger should be clear. What is happening in black America today merely foreshadows the full force inherent in the rise of the managerial estate. Not only will the question "Who needs the Negro?" be voiced with greater frequency, but the question: "Who *is* needed and who *is* not?" will be applied broadly across the entire population. The answers are likely to be as chilling as the question.

## Notes

1. See, e.g., Race Differences in Earnings: A Survey and New Evidence, by J.P. Smith and F. Welch, published in March, 1978, by the Rand Corporation of Santa Monica, CA; and *Closing the Gap: Forty Years of Economic Progress for Blacks*, by the same authors, published in February 1986, by the Rand Corporation. Smith and Welch contend that black "gains" are due to improvements in the quality and quantity of black education and blacks' transition from southern, mainly agricultural, labor to northern industrial wage labor. In another article by Smith and Welch, entitled Black Economic Progress After Myrdal, published in the *Journal of Economic Literature, 27*, in June 1989, they acknowledge that South-to-North migration no longer serves as a vehicle for black economic gain.

2. For a compact and thorough critique of the optimistic reading, see J.P. Cotton's article Some Observations of Closing the Gap, published in the *Trotter Institute Review, 1* (1), Winter 1987, by the William Monroe Trotter Institute, University of Massachusetts at Boston, pages 13-16; and Cotton's article Opening the Gap, which is forthcoming in the *Social Science Quarterly*.

3. In an excellent recent survey of these issues J.J. Heckman has complained that the Darity-Myers assumption that nonworkers make zero earnings is "extreme." Still, as the econometrician who has done the basic research on selection bias problems, he long has argued that the labor force dropout phenomenon has biased the data on black-white differences toward an optimistic reading. He seems to place more credence in C. Brown's finding that two-thirds of the measured black gain for males is due to underaccounting for poor blacks. See J.J. Heckman's article The Impact of Government on the Economic Status of Black Americans in *The Question of Discrimination*, edited by S. Shulman and W. Darity, Jr., published in 1989, by Wesleyan University Press, Middletown, CT.

4. For the classic analysis, see E.F. Frazier's *The Negro Family in the United States*, published in 1939 by the University of Chicago Press.

5. See W. Darity, Jr.'s, article The Managerial Class and Industrial Policy, published in *Industrial Relations, 25* (2), Spring 1986, pages 212-27; and also Darity's article The Managerial Class and Surplus Population, published in *Society, 21* (1), November-December 1983, pages 54-62. For an earlier classic discussion of the managerial class that differs from Darity's, see T. Kemp's article The Intelligentsia and Modern Capitalism, published in *Science and Society, 26* (3), Summer 1962, pages 309-325.

6. It is anecdotal, but telling nonetheless, that typically no black-owned business on the *Black Enterprise* top 100 list comes close to making the *Fortune* 500 list.

7. In his book *Black Bourgeoisie*, published in 1957 by The Free Press, Glencoe, IL, E.F. Frazier made the following comment during the era of enforced segregation:

> Since the black bourgeoisie is composed chiefly of white-collar workers and since its small business enterprises are insignificant in the American economy, the black bourgeoisie wields no political power as a class in American society. Nor does the black bourgeoisie exercise any significant power within the Negro community as an employer of labor. Its power within the Negro community stems from the fact that middle-class Negroes hold strategic positions in segregated institutions and create and propagate the ideologies current in the Negro community. (p. 86)

As will be shown, although desegregation has come quite a distance, the black bourgeoisie still has the same functional position.

8. In his book *Black Bourgeoisie*, E.F. Frazier highlights the Rosenwald Fund as a major example of northern industrial philanthropy.

9. For example, sociologist W.D. Rubinstein reports in *The Left, the Right, and the Jews*, published in 1982 by Universe Books, New York, that since 1945 almost the entire Jewish population in the United States and throughout the western world has entered "the upper-middle class." The intra-ethnic class stratification among Jewish Americans thus stands in sharp contrast with that of black Americans. (pp. 11-76)

10. See B. Woody and M. Malson, In Crisis: Low Income Black Employed Women in the U.S. Workplace, Working Paper No. 131, published by Wellesley College, Wellesley, MA in 1984; and W. Darity, Jr., and S.L. Myers, Jr., Changes in Black Family Structure: Implications for Welfare Dependency, published in the *American Economic Review: AEA Papers and Proceedings*, May 1983.

11. See the substantial critical assessment of New Industrial Policy by R. McGahey and J. Jeffries in Employment, Training, and Industrial Policy: Implications for Minorities, a paper prepared for the Joint Center on Political Studies Conference on Industrial Policy and Minority Economic Opportunity, October 13-14, 1983.

12. For a detailed analysis of the role of seniority arrangements and other union procedures as racially exclusionary tactics both in the public and private sector, see H. Hill, The Racial Practices of Organized Labor: The Contemporary Record, in J. Jacobson (Ed.), *The Negro and the American Labor Market*, published in 1968 by Anchor Books, Garden City, NJ; and H. Hill, The Equal Employment Opportunity Acts of 1964 and 1972: A Critical Analysis of the Legislative History and Administration of the Law, published in the *Industrial Relations Law Journal*, 2 (1) Spring 1977; and H. Hill, *Black Labor and the American Legal System*, published in 1986 by University of Wisconsin Press, Madison, WI.

13. In New York City six out of ten students do not complete high school in four years.

14. Data obtained from the University of Illinois at Chicago.

15. Data obtained from the University of North Carolina at Chapel Hill.

16. Of course, it is not clear when blacks as a group ever were "empowered" in the United States.

17. See D.K. Magner's article Decline in Doctorates Earned by Black and White Men Persists, Study Finds; Foreign Students and U.S. Women Fill Gaps, published March 1, 1989, in *The Chronicle of Higher Education*. In the same article, C. Smith, Dean of Graduate Studies at Florida A & M University is quoted as observing that "The black male appears to be in a dangerous state of decline in both academics and society."

# References

Associated Press. (1987, December 29). Black Enrollments in Graduate Schools Drop, Study Says. *Durham Morning Herald*.

Bluestone, B. & Harrison, B. (1986, December). *The Great American Job Machine: The Proliferation of Low Wage Employment in the U.S. Economy*. Washington, DC: The Joint Economic Committee.

Bradbury, K.L. & Browne, L.E. (1986, March/April). Black Men in the Labor Market. *New England Economic Review*, 32-42.

Brown, C. (1982). The Federal Attack on Labor Market Discrimination: The Mouse That Roared. *Research in Labor Economics*, 5, 60.

Brown, M.K. & Erie, S.P. (1981, Summer). Blacks and the Legacy of the Great Society: The Economic and Political Impact of Federal Social Policy. *Public Policy*, 308-309.

Bunche, R.J. (1936, January). A Critique of New Deal Social Planning As It Affects Negroes. *Journal of Negro Education*, 62, 65.

Clark, K.B. & Franklin, J.H. (1983). Forward to *Policy Framework for Social Justice*. Washington, DC: Joint Center for Political Studies.

Clark, L.H., Jr. (1986, December 4). Productivity's Cost: Manufacturers Grow Much More Efficient But Employment Lags. *The Wall Street Journal*.

Coe, R.D. (1982, September/October). Welfare Dependence: Fact or Myth? *Challenge*, 25 (4), 43-49.

Coleman, M. (1983, December 4). More Reliant on Aid than Whites, Blacks Hit Hard by Cuts. *The Washington Post*, p. A1.

Darity, W., Jr. (1980, Winter). Illusions of Black Economic Progress. *The Review of Black Political Economy*, 153-168.

Darity, W., Jr. (1983, November-December). The Managerial Class and Surplus Population. *Society*, 21, (1).

Darity, W., Jr. (1986, Spring). The Managerial Class and Industrial Policy. *Industrial Relations*, 25 (2), 212-227.

Darity, W., Jr. & Myers, S.L., Jr. (1980, Summer). Changes in Black-White Income Inequality, 1968-1978: A Decade of Progress? *The Review of Black Political Economy*, 10 (4), 355-374.

Darity, W., Jr. & Myers, S.L., Jr. (1984, Fall). Public Policy and the Condition of Black Family Life. *Review of Black Political Economy*, 12 (1-2), 165-187.

Duvall, J. (1987, October 31). New Organization Seeks to Be Voice of Black Professors. *The Carolina Times*, pp. 1, 4.

Frazier, E.F. (1957). *Black Bourgeoisie*. Glencoe, IL: The Free Press.

Freeman, R.B. (1973). Changes in the Labor Market for Black Americans, 1948-72. *Brookings Papers on Economic Activity 1*.

Freeman, R.B. (1983). *Who Escapes? The Relation of Church-Going and Other Background Factors to the Socio-Economic Performance of Black Male Youths from Inner City Poverty Tracts*. Paper prepared for the NBER Conference on Inner City Black Youth Unemployment, August 11-12, 1983.

Garg, D. (1986, December). *The Impact of Automation and Computer-Integrated Manufacturing on Industrial Employment*. Paper presented at the annual meeting of the American Society of Mechanical Engineers.

*Gomillion v. Lighfoot*, 364 U.S. 399, 110 (1960).

Hogan, L.M. (1972, Fall). Review of Wilhelm's Who Needs the Negro? *Review of Black Political Economy, 3* (1).

Jacques-Garvey, A. (Ed.). (1977) *Philosophy and Opinions of Marcus Garvey*, 2 vols. New York: Atheneum.

Leontief, W. & Duchin, F. (1986). *The Future of Automation on Workers*. New York: Oxford University Press.

Mandel, E. (1980). *Long Waves of Capitalist Development: The Marxist Interpretation*. Cambridge: Cambridge University Press.

Marx, K. (1977). *Capital*, Volume 1. New York: Vintage Books, pp. 784-794.

McGhee, J.D. (1982). *A Dream Denied: The Black Family in the Eighties*. Washington, DC: National Urban League Research Department.

McLanahan, S. (1985). Family Structure and Reproduction of Poverty. *American Journal of Sociology, 90*, 873-901.

Michael, D.N. (1962). *Cybernation: The Silent Conquest*. Santa Barbara: Center for the Study of Democratic Institutions.

Nora, S. & Minc, A. (1978). *The Computerization of Society: A Report to the President of France*. Cambridge, MA: MIT Press.

Rada, J. (1980). *The Impact of Micro-Electronics: A Tentative Appraisal of Information Technology*. Geneva: International Labor Office.

Reis, D. (1987, May). Minorities on Slow Tenure Track at Chicago Area Universities. *Chicago Reviewer*, 3-5.

Shaw, L.B. (1982). High School Completions for Young Women: Impacts of Low Income and Living with a Single Parent. *Journal of Family Issues, 3*, 147-163.

Silberman, C. (1966). *The Myths of Automation*. New York: Harper Colophon Books.

Smith, J.P. & Welch, F. (1986, February). *Closing the Gap: Forty Years of Economic Progress for Blacks*. Santa Monica: The Rand Corporation.

Smith, J.P. & Welch, F. (1989, June). Black Economic Progress After Myrdal. *Journal of Economic Literature, 27* (2), 561.

Taylor, P.A., Gwartney-Gibbs, P.A., & Farley, R. (1986). Changes in the Structure of Earnings Inequality by Race, Sex, and Industrial Sector, 1960-80. *Research in Social Stratification and Mobility, 5*, 105-138.

U.S. Bureau of the Census. (1983a). *Characterization of the Population Below the Poverty Level: 1981*. Current Population Reports Series P-60 No. 138. Washington, DC: U.S. Government Printing Office.

U.S. Bureau of the Census. (1983b). *Money Income of Households, Families and Persons in the United States; 1981*. Current Population Reports Series P-60 No. 137. Washington, DC: U.S. Government Printing Office.

Wilhelm, S.M. (1970). *Who Needs the Negro?* Cambridge, MA: Schenkman Publishing.

Wilson, W.J. (1980). *The Declining Significance of Race* (2nd ed.). Chicago: University of Chicago Press.

# 3

# Black Political Participation: The Search for Power

### E. Yvonne Moss

Black political participation during the period 1940 to the present can be best understood as a search for power. Using both conventional and nonconventional politics, African-Americans sought inclusion, full participation, and effective representation in the nation's power centers and political arenas. Until the Voting Rights Act of 1965 secured the franchise for millions of African-Americans in the South and in some jurisdictions in the North and West, black political participation took unconventional forms including protests and political movements. Protests and demonstrations played a pivotal role in the political and social advancement of black Americans. African-Americans turned to these nonconventional political methods because the basic political relationship of black citizens to the polity was one of exclusion.

The politics of exclusion meant that African-Americans lacked access to political institutions and processes. Supreme Court interpretations of the Civil War Amendments to the Constitution and the civil rights laws and cases of the nineteenth century so emasculated these measures that black people were denied even the basic rights of citizenship that these amendments and laws were supposed to guarantee. Concomitantly, patterns of bias developed within the structures of politics that automatically disadvantaged black citizens (Harrigan, 1985; Fainstein and Fainstein, 1974; and Katznelson, 1976, 1981). African-Americans were excluded from the power centers and bargaining arenas where public agendas were set and public policies determined. Disfranchisement in the South and dilution of power in both the North and West meant that the only avenues available for black political participation were accommodation, coalition, or confrontation (Carmichael and Hamilton, 1967; Greenberg, Milner, and Olson, 1971; Holden, 1973). The routine organization of race politics in the United States either excluded black participation or linked black citizens to the polity in a way that minimized their potential influence (Katznelson, 1976). Faced with a closed political system that was reinforced by de facto and de jure structures of segregation, African-Americans turned to agitation, litigation, and various nonviolent direct-action techniques to end segregation, second-class citizenship, and disfranchisement. The protests, demonstrations, and political violence of the sixties were the forms of political mobilizations that assumed importance after World War II. (Greenberg, Milner, and Olson, 1971; Carson, 1981; Raines, 1983; Morris, 1984; Sears and McConahay, 1973; Miroff, 1979; Neiburg, 1969; Zinn, 1964).

Between 1940 and the late 1960s, the political aspirations of black Americans were expressed in mass popular movements for civil rights and for black power. The diverse group of leaders and organizations known collectively as the civil rights movement encompassed different political philosophies and orientations. Sometimes leaders and organizations initiated protest activity, but more often it was their role to give shape and direction to spontaneous popular sentiment and behavior (Morris, 1984; Raines, 1983; Carson, 1981). The civil rights movement was technically a sociopolitical movement in that it had both social and political objectives. As the emphasis shifted from the desegregation of public facilities to voter registration and political participation, there was an increasing awareness that finding solutions to social and economic ills required the gaining of political power (Carson, 1981; Carmichael and Hamilton, 1967; Meier, 1970; Breitman, 1967; and King, 1968).

Prior to the emergence of the civil rights movement terror and intimidation had long been used to reinforce economic, social, and political exclusion and domination.[1] It was used to frighten African-Americans into acquiescence and into acceptance of the political order. Doctrines of white supremacy were a part of a political culture that justified exclusion on the basis of race. The brash militancy of some of the civil rights activists, the defiant and accusatory rhetoric of Malcolm X, the confrontational rhetoric of black power and the appeals to black nationalism, religious nationalism, and revolutionary nationalism, all functioned to counteract fear by generating a new group consciousness and identity. Issues of power and powerlessness were raised in both religious and secular terms. The political violence of the sixties, along with the black power movement, are direct reactions to the politics of exclusion (U.S. Kerner Commission, 1968; Sears and McConahay, 1973; Neiburg, 1969; Button, 1978).

After 1965 black political mobilization was channeled more and more into electoral politics and conventional political behavior. Even so, nonconventional political activity–especially political movements–continued. Rent strikes and poor people's campaigns, the black power movement, urban political movements for community control, rural and urban movements for economic development and self-sufficiency, and political mobilization to elect black candidates are all examples of nonconventional political behavior on the part of black people in the late sixties and seventies (Altshuler, 1970; Lipsky, 1980; Fainstein and Fainstein, 1974; Piven and Cloward, 1977; James, 1973; Meier, 1970; Katznelson, 1981). Early campaigns to elect black mayors and other public officials relied to a considerable extent on nonconventional modes of political mobilization among black citizens.

Black political ascendancy and the transition to black rule in the cities has been the most visible result of black participation in conventional politics (Moss, 1977; Eisinger, 1980). However, progress in black empowerment is evident in other political arenas and levels of government as well. This chapter examines the gradual evolution of conventional black political participation, primarily through an evaluation of the developments in black registration and voting from the forties to the present. It also raises questions about the impact of increased black voting behavior and identifies the consequences of and the major issues associated with these developments.

Additionally, the chapter discusses the political context of African-American politics, as well as pertinent theoretical issues regarding the structure of power.

The final section addresses the following questions: Why haven't increased black political participation, generally, and black political ascendancy in the cities, particularly, produced improvements in the economic and social lives of more African-Americans? What are the limits and what is the potential of political participation for the realization of black aspirations? What directions for political action are indicated by the study? And, where do we go from here?

This chapter has a number of objectives: to review the trends in black registration and voting from 1940 to the present; to evaluate the impact and significance of black voting; to address the role and function of political movements; to examine the myths and realities of ideological differentiation in black populations; to describe the political context within which the search for power continues to take place; and, to evaluate why this search continues. A discussion of context is critical because black political activity takes place within the general structure and dynamics of American politics. Two key elements are the structure of race politics and the structure of power. Any comprehensive analysis of black politics and black political potential must take into consideration the relationship between black politics and the larger political context.

## Trends in Black Registration and Voting

In this section the trends in black registration and voting from 1940 to the present will be reviewed. One limitation of this project is that as we go back in time we have less information, so our trend data are incomplete and uneven. We do, however, have enough data to make some solid generalizations. The evidence on black registration, turnout, and vote preference will be discussed.

Table 3-1 presents data on black voter registration in the South from 1940 to 1973. One shortcoming of the registration data by race is that they are only available for the South. Several points are worth noting about this data. First, there was a 140% increase in black registration from 1940 to 1947, attributable largely to the ending of the white primary[2] (*Smith v. Allwright*) in 1944 (Walton, 1985). Second, black registration gains were steady, albeit slow, from 1947 until 1964, but there was a tremendous increase between 1964 and 1968, obviously a result of the passage of the Voting Rights Act of 1965.

A more detailed impact of this law can be seen in table 3-2. This table contains voter registration figures for the South immediately prior to and after the Voting Rights Act. The table's only limitation for our purposes is that it lists these figures for whites and nonwhites, rather than whites and blacks. However, since blacks constituted the overwhelming number of nonwhites in these states, this is not a serious limitation. These results are quite clear: overall, nonwhite registration increased from 35.5% to 57.2% of the voting age population, an increase of over 60% in only a

## Table 3-1

Black Voter Registration in the South, 1940-1973

| Year | Estimated Number of Registered | Percentage of Black Voting Age Population |
|------|-------------------------------|-------------------------------------------|
| 1940 | 250,000 | 5 |
| 1947 | 595,000 | 12 |
| 1952 | 1,008,614 | 20 |
| 1956 | 1,238,038 | 25 |
| 1960 | 1,414,052 | 28 |
| 1964 | 1,907,279 | 38 |
| 1968 | 3,312,000 | 62 |
| 1970 | 3,357,000 | 54 |
| 1971 | 3,488,565 | 59 |
| 1973 | 3,560,856 | 59 |

Source: Black Politics in the South, by D. Campbell and J.R. Feagin, 1975, *Journal of Politics, 37*, p. 133.

## Table 3-2

Voter Registration in the South, Prior to and After the Voting Rights Act of 1965

| State | Pre-Act Registration Percentage | | % Point Difference[a] | Post-Act Registration Percentage | | % Point Difference[a] |
|---|---|---|---|---|---|---|
| | White | Nonwhite | | White | Nonwhite | |
| Alabama | 69.2 | 19.3 | 49.9 | 89.6 | 51.6 | 38.0 |
| Arkansas | 65.5 | 40.4 | 25.1 | 72.4 | 62.8 | 9.6 |
| Florida | 74.8 | 51.2 | 23.6 | 81.4 | 63.6 | 17.6 |
| Georgia | 62.6 | 27.4 | 35.2 | 80.3 | 52.6 | 27.7 |
| Louisiana | 80.5 | 31.6 | 48.9 | 93.1 | 58.9 | 34.2 |
| Mississippi | 69.9 | 6.7 | 63.2 | 91.5 | 59.8 | 31.7 |
| North Carolina | 96.8 | 46.8 | 50.0 | 83.0 | 51.3 | 31.7 |
| South Carolina | 75.7 | 37.3 | 38.4 | 81.7 | 51.2 | 30.5 |
| Tennessee | 72.9 | 69.5 | 3.4 | 80.6 | 71.7 | 8.9 |
| Texas | .... | .... | .... | 53.3 | 61.6 | -8.3 |
| Virginia | 61.1 | 38.3 | 22.8 | 63.4 | 55.6 | 7.8 |
| Total | 73.4 | 35.5 | 37.9 | 76.5 | 57.2 | 19.3 |

[a]Prepared by author.
Source: *Political Participation* (pp. 222-23), by U.S. Commission on Civil Rights, 1968, Washington, DC: Government Printing Office.

few years. Yet large gaps remain between nonwhite and white rates even after 1965. While the registration rate of whites in all southern states only increased from 73.4% to 76.5% prior to and after the Voting Rights Act of 1965, in 6 of the 11 southern states, whites registered at a rate approximately 30% higher than blacks. In one state, Tennessee, the percentage of increase in white voter registration was greater than that for blacks.

Since 1968 the U.S. Census Bureau has compiled registration and voting statistics broken down by various social groups for every national election. We have reproduced these for blacks and whites for the presidential elections from 1964 to 1984 (table 3-3). Black registration has remained remarkably stable through this period, starting out at 66.2% (1968), dropping in 1976 to 58.5%, but then rebounding to 66.3% in 1984. During the same time, white voter registration has decreased from 75.4% to 69.6%. Thus, the ratio of black registration to white registration increased from .88 to .95, an indication of the convergence of registration rates between blacks and whites.

Tables 3-3 and 3-4 contain figures on black voter turnout. In this presentation we are restricting our attention to voting in presidential elections because the greatest amount of information is available on these and they have been the most common focus of political analysts. For information on voting in other elections, see Hanes Walton's *Invisible Politics* (1985, chap. 5). The data in table 3-3 come from the Census Bureau, while those in table 3-4 are from the American National Election Studies Project (ANES) conducted by the University of Michigan. As has been discussed elsewhere (Wolfinger and Rosenstone, 1980), the estimates from these two sources disagree, with the ANES data tending to overreport voting. We ask the reader to bear this in mind when noting the differences between these two sets of results.

This having been said, the ANES data (table 3-4) is the best for examining black turnout prior to 1968, even though it includes a relatively small number of blacks in each survey (Walton, 1985). From this data, we can see that black turnout in presidential elections hovered around 33% during the 1950s, increased dramatically to 52.9% in 1960 and then to 64.9% in 1964, and has remained relatively stable since then. This masks the change in the South, however, where turnout among blacks increased from 4% in 1952 to 31% in 1960 and 63% in 1968 (Cassel, 1979). Similar trends, although at lower levels of reported voting, are found in the census data (table 3-3).

In addition to the data on turnout, we have figures on the presidential preferences of blacks. Most of this data is based on the ANES surveys, and therefore only covers the period from 1952 to 1984 (table 3-5). What we know about black voting from 1940 until 1948 indicates that blacks voted overwhelmingly Democratic during these three elections (Glantz, 1960). And, as is well-known and is documented in table 3-5, this trend has continued to the present. Essentially, the conclusion that can be drawn from the turnout and preference data is that in presidential elections blacks either vote Democrat or do not vote at all.

## Table 3-3

### National Registration and Voting by Race, 1964-1984

|  | 1964 | 1968 | 1972 | 1976 | 1980 | 1984 |
|---|---|---|---|---|---|---|
| **Blacks** | | | | | | |
| Percentage of voting-age population reported registered | NA | 66.2% | 65.5% | 58.5% | 60.0% | 66.3% |
| Percentage of voting-age population reported voting | 58.5% | 57.6% | 52.1% | 48.7% | 50.5% | 55.8% |
| **Whites** | | | | | | |
| Percentage of voting-age population reported registered | NA | 75.4% | 73.4% | 68.3% | 68.6% | 69.6% |
| Percentage of voting-age population reported voting | 70.7% | 69.1% | 64.5% | 60.9% | 61.1% | 61.4% |

Source: *Current Population Reports, Special Studies*, U.S. Bureau of the Census, Series P-23, No. 131.

## Table 3-4

Reported Voter Turnout by Race for Presidential Elections, 1952-1984

|       | 1952 | 1956 | 1960 | 1964 | 1968 | 1972 | 1976 | 1980 | 1984 |
|-------|------|------|------|------|------|------|------|------|------|
| White | 78.5 | 76.5 | 81.9 | 79.6 | 77.1 | 73.8 | 72.5 | 72.3 | 75.2 |
| Black | 33.1 | 34.9 | 52.9 | 64.9 | 67.7 | 64.7 | 65.0 | 66.7 | 65.6 |

Source: Data for 1952 to 1978 from *American National Election Studies Data Sourcebook, 1952-1978* (p. 317), by W.E. Miller, A.H. Miller, and E.J. Schneider; 1980, Cambridge: Harvard University Press. Data for 1980, 1982, and 1984 from American National Election Studies, Center for Political Studies, University of Michigan.

## Table 3-5

Percent Democratic Vote in Presidential Elections, 1952-1984

|        | 1952 | 1956 | 1960 | 1964 | 1968 | 1972 | 1976 | 1980 | 1984 |
|--------|------|------|------|------|------|------|------|------|------|
| Blacks | 80   | 64   | 71   | 100  | 97   | 87   | 95   | 86   | 91   |
| Whites | 40   | 39   | 48   | 65   | 41   | 30   | 47   | 36   | 33   |

Source: Data for 1952 to 1976 from *American National Election Studies Data Sourcebook, 1952-1978*, by W.E. Miller, A.H. Miller, and E.J. Schneider; 1980, Cambridge: Harvard University Press. Data for 1980 to 1984 cited in *The Social Basis of Politics* by A.K. Sherman and A. Kolker, 1987, Belmont, CA: Wadsworth.

The increases in black participation in electoral politics should be viewed within a political context in which there have been major barriers to registration and voting. Any impediment to registration, obviously enough, is also an impediment to voting. The reverse is not true, however. Even when black citizens are registered, obstacles to effective and meaningful voting can be devised (e.g., racial gerrymandering; see Parker, 1984). During the years between 1940 and 1987 there were five general types of barriers used to inhibit full participation of black voters in electoral contests. These included legal or procedural barriers, illegal barriers, the effects of socioeconomic status, psychological factors and organizational factors, and the residual consequences of the political culture. Legal or procedural barriers include pre-1965 mechanisms that resulted in disfranchisement, such as the white primary, poll taxes, and literacy tests. Since 1965 other methods have been used to discourage registration and voting among African-Americans, including: difficult registration requirements; frequent purges of registration rolls; moving polling places with little or no notice; and reducing the number of polling places within black residential areas (Davidson, 1984, p. 3).

One illustration of the impact of registration rules is evident from Wolfinger and Rosenston's study, *Who Votes?* (1980). Based on 1972 data they estimated that if all states had registration procedures as simple and accessible as the most liberal state, turnout for whites would have increased by 8.9% and for blacks by 11.3%. It is apparent that the nature and type of registration requirements employed in the U.S. depresses the turnout of blacks more than that of whites.

After the passage of the Voting Rights Act in 1965 the key question was no longer whether African-Americans could participate in conventional politics, but rather what the terms of that participation would be. Since 1965 the kinds of limitations on black political participation used during the machine era in northern and midwestern cities (Katznelson, 1976) have been increasingly used in other jurisdictions to constrain black political potential. Just as the structure of race politics during the machine era (in places like New York and Chicago) and during the progressive era (Fainstein and Fainstein, 1974; Harrigan, 1985) limited the effectiveness of black political participation, so after 1965 in the South, new mechanisms were tried to limit the political potential of black voters who registered and began voting in record numbers.

Other mechanisms do not actually prevent blacks from voting, but rather dilute the political impact of the black vote (Bell, 1980). Since the importance of one's vote increases turnout (Zipp, 1985), these mechanisms have the effect of being an obstacle to effective black voting. These obstacles have become more important since the Voting Rights Act of 1965 eliminated many of the outright barriers to actual participation by blacks. These methods include at-large elections, gerrymandering, antisingle shot devices, annexation of predominately white areas, and runoff requirements that stipulate that no candidate can be elected without 50% of the vote (Davidson, 1984; Davidson and Korbel, 1981; Parker, 1984; Walton, 1985). From 1964 to 1975, 20 county governments and boards of education changed from district-based to at-large elections (Voter Education Project, 1976). Many of these changes occurred in southern states (Davidson, 1984, pp. 11-12).

The effects of these changes on minority vote dilution can be assessed by drawing on Davidson and Korbel's (1981) study of political units in Texas that changed from at-large to ward-based systems during the 1970s. They found that the number of elected officials who were African-American or Mexican-American was three times greater under ward-based systems. Furthermore, there is evidence that southern states covered by the Voting Rights Act have increasingly requested the sorts of changes in electoral procedures (at-large elections, annexations, changes in polling places) that dilute black voting strength, and that there is a positive relationship between the number of black elected officials and the number of such requests (Hunter, 1974; U.S. Commission on Civil Rights, 1982). Similarly, southern states have often failed to submit these changes for preclearance, as is required by law. The U.S. Commission on Civil Rights concluded that there were over 500 election law changes that were not submitted for preclearance in Alabama, Georgia, and Mississippi alone (Simpson and Yinger, 1985, p. 231). In some states (Georgia, Mississippi, and South Carolina), when requests for such changes were denied, state officials managed to implement them through other means (Davidson, 1984, p. 12).

Illegal barriers to both registration and voting have also been used to restrict the use of the franchise by black citizens. The history of these prior to 1965 is well-known and includes such things as the threat and/or use of violence, economic harm, verbal abuse, and, most prevalently, arbitrary registration procedures (e.g., the closing of doors as soon as blacks attempted to register). Investigations by the U.S. Commission on Civil Rights concluded that such discriminatory practices were concentrated in 129 counties in 10 southern states (U.S. Commission on Civil Rights, 1959; 1961).

After 1965, local southern officials continued to erect roadblocks to black registration and voting. Frequently the same white registrars who were hostile to blacks prior to the Voting Rights Act remained in office after its passage. Again, arbitrary procedures were used to hinder blacks. Registration places were changed and blacks were purged from registration rolls without notice. Posted office hours were not kept. If blacks did register, they faced problems in actually voting. Common practices included failing to list the black voter on the precinct list or, if listed, failing to locate his or her name on election day; harassing black voters when they tried to cast their ballots; and refusing to allow blacks to vote without verification of their eligibility from city hall (U.S. Commission on Civil Rights, 1975).

Conventional wisdom dictates that higher socioeconomic status (SES) is positively related to voting (Milbrath and Goel, 1977). The argument is that a person with a higher SES is better integrated into society, has a better education which allows for more effective processing of political information, and is more aware of the need for and the benefits of political participation (Lipset, 1963; Verba and Nie, 1972). Contrary to these conventional concepts, black citizens with low SES are more likely to vote than whites with low SES (Olsen, 1970; Verba and Nie, 1972, pp. 170-

1). Two different explanations have been offered for this. One is that blacks are more "group conscious" than whites and that this consciousness moves blacks to participate in politics (Verba and Nie, 1972, pp. 158-9). A second explanation holds that blacks are more tied to the community and that this tie prompts political participation (Olsen, 1970). The work of Danigelis (1978), who tested these assumptions, and Walton (1985) indicates that it is primarily structural factors that influence black voter turnout. The most important of these is the "political climate"–whether the electoral structure is supportive, intolerant, or indifferent in respect to black political participation. Black voters turn out in higher numbers regardless of SES when they have something or someone to vote for, and when structural factors are not a barrier to voting.

It is not clear what role psychological factors such as fear, apathy, and deference to whites–which historically have had an impact on black voting patterns–have today (Salaman and Van Evera, 1973; Kernell, 1973). Organizational factors, however, are clearly related to black registration and voting. The reluctance of political parties to nominate and support black candidates for office has a chilling effect on black participation. On the other hand, the presence of black candidates and federal registrars is significantly related to black political mobilization (Walton, 1985, p. 76). Voters' perceptions that a particular candidate represents their interests increases turnout (Zipp, 1985). And in city races the presence of black mayoral candidates increases black voter turnouts (Morris, 1984). In presidential politics, Jesse Jackson's bid for the Democratic nomination generally increased black registration and voting (Reed, 1986). For example, in Alabama, there was an 87% increase; in New York, the increase was a dramatic 127%.

Historically, the evolution of a political culture that legitimized the exclusion of African-Americans from the political life of the country politically neutralized black citizens (Walton, 1985). With disfranchisement black people lost more than the right to vote. What was also lost were the political benefits that accrue from suffrage rights, such as employment opportunities and the improvement of schools and services. In 1880 African-Americans were a majority in 300 counties in the United States. By 1970 that number was down to 100. It is interesting to surmise what the impact on black life might have been if political inclusion rather than political exclusion had been the norm in American politics from the 1880s onward.

## Impact of Black Voting

While the impact of black registration and voting during the years 1940 to 1987 has been considerable, controversy remains over whether greater participation in politics can change the material conditions of most African-Americans. The Voting Rights Act of 1965 created the opportunity for millions of black people to register and vote without harassment, threats, or fears of reprisals. This accomplishment is of historical importance because for the first time in the nation's history black Americans began to enjoy some of the benefits of citizenship. Black voters have helped to elect blacks to public office, as well as whites who are sympathetic to black interests. Even though black elected officials (BEOs) represented only 1.2% of the total number of elected officials in the United States (490,770) in 1984, there was a 300% increase in the number of BEOs between 1970 and 1985, from 1,469 to 6,065 (Williams, 1987). While there were fewer than 300 BEOs in the country in 1965, by 1987 there were 6,681 (Boamah-Waife, 1990).

These gains, however, are not reflected at all levels of government. The greatest inroads have been at the county level, while the election of black candidates to state offices has been the least successful. Virginia's recent election of the nation's first black elected governor was, therefore, especially historic. There are currently no black representatives in the U.S. Senate and only a few in Congress. In addition to the nation's one black governor, there are a few state officials who are black. Some of the nation's black members of Congress, as well as black lobbying organizations and black party officials, have gained positions of influence in American political institutions. Even so, some scholars conclude that electoral success has not located black Americans in real positions of power.

In recent years the number of BEOs has declined. Since traditionally the most critical determinant of electoral success is the percentage of blacks voting in a district—the election of BEOs in districts with black people representing less than 40% of the population is not common—the number of blacks elected to office would seem to be limited by the number of majority or near-majority black districts in the United States. There is, however, evidence to support the conclusion that the presence of black voters makes an impact even when black officeholders are not elected. A sizable block of black voters influences the political agendas of candidates and elected officials. For example, there was a decline in the segregationist rhetoric in southern gubernatorial races after the increase in black voter participation (Black, 1976). Concomitantly, white members of Congress who have a sizable black population in their districts have been supporters of civil rights legislation (Bass and DeVries, 1976; Feagin, 1972).

While the election of black officials, especially big-city mayors, is a limited political resource for addressing certain kinds of political issues—like the economic inequality between blacks and whites—BEOs have had some positive impact on the distribution of services to black members of the polity. One of these areas is the increase in the proportion of black municipal employment. In a study of 40 cities, Eisinger (1983) concluded that the presence of a black mayor was one of the most important reasons for the growth of black municipal employment in the 1970s. In his study of Durham, North Carolina, and Tuskegee, Alabama, Keech (1968) found that black voting resulted in greater black public employment and a fairer distribution of public services. Similar conclusions concerning the positive impact of black elected officials have been reported by Campbell and Feagin (1975), Coombs, et al. (1977), Greer (1979), Karnig and Welch (1980), and Marshall and Tabb (1985).

Some argue that increases in black municipal employment have primarily benefited members of the black middle class. Additionally, the increase in black political power in major cities in the United States has taken place at a time when the power of cities to affect significant changes in the social structure has decreased (Williams, 1987). Changes in urban political structures have limited the power of city government officials to affect social change. Black mayors are not able to provide the benefits to their constituents that ethnic mayors in political machines traditionally were able to provide. Thus, participation does not bring the power it once did to affect issues of social mobility. Despite the limitations inherent in the contemporary organization of politics in the United States, both the dramatic increase in the number of BEOs since 1965 and the transition to black rule in the nation's largest cities denote critical rather than routine changes in the structure of racial politics in America.[3]

Voting by itself is a limited political resource. The fact that over 6,209,000 black Americans remained unregistered in 1987 further limits voting potential. Nevertheless, black voters are becoming more sophisticated in utilizing the power of the vote to reward friends and to punish enemies whether they are black or white. Although the actual black registration and voter turnout lags behind the potential, scholars still find reason for optimism. The gap between voter registration rates for black and white citizens narrowed to 3.3% points in 1984 from 9.2% points in 1968 (see table 3-3). The gap in voter turnout narrowed from 10.4% points in 1980 to 5.6% points in 1984 (see table 3-3). The steady increase in the numbers of BEOs since 1965 is likely to increase even with a limited number of majority black districts. Such an increase is possible if black candidates capture larger shares of the votes of other racial groups (including whites), if black voter registration and turnout is increased, and if the structural barriers to effective political participation among African-Americans are reduced or eliminated.

There has been a long-standing debate concerning voting as a source of social change. Is social change best accomplished by devoting one's energies to electing candidates who represent one's interest, or is it best to remain outside the electoral arena and use one's resources to build social movements or to engage in related activities (Piven and Cloward, 1977)? This debate has had a long history within the black movement. Some analysts have questioned whether social problems could ever be solved through the vote (e.g., Brown, 1969; Jones, 1972; and Greenberg, Milner, and Olson, 1971). On the other hand, Dr. Martin Luther King, Jr., said in 1965 that if blacks could vote "there would be no oppressive poverty directed against Negroes, our children would not be crippled by segregated schools, and the whole community might live together in harmony" (Herbes, 1965). Other writers (Greeley, 1971; Levy and Kramer, 1972) have voiced similar positions. Perhaps the safest conclusion is to point out the debate and to note that voting, by itself, has limited political power.

Focusing only on conventional political participation may also be misleading because central to any analysis of black politics is the general question of politics and power.[4] Many political and social scientists have studied political participation from the pluralist viewpoint. The assumption is that voting has a substantial impact not only on who holds office but also on public policy. It is further assumed that the range of issues subject to debate by elected officials is not significantly narrower than all the concerns that confront a given polity. This view ignores the fact that some issues never come up for debate (Bachrach and Baratz, 1970). Those who hold the power of nondecisions in public agenda-setting often do not hold public office, are little known to the public, and are seldom accountable to public interests (Bachrach and Baratz, 1962). As Alford and Friedland (1975) noted, some groups (e.g., the upper classes) have power without participating in politics, while others (e.g., the lower classes) can actively participate yet not have power.

Schattschneider (1960), Dolbeare and Edelman (1981), Katznelson and Kesselman (1987), Greenberg (1986), Parenti (1970b, 1983), Hunter (1953), Mills (1956), and Dye (1979) all contradict and call into question the pluralist model of politics and power in America. And, even if one accepts the pluralist model, there are built-in limits and impediments to full participation by black citizens in conventional pluralist politics (Greenberg, Milner, and Olson 1971). Greenberg's comments made almost 20 years ago have contemporary applicability:

> Recall that under the pluralist model some questions remain outside the boundaries of legitimate political discourse and decision making. Communities seem to reach a decision, whether explicitly or implicitly, that some concerns and related solutions are not proper subject matter for the political arena. Unfortunately, many questions considered closed by the majority of the community are often of vital importance to Black citizens. William Keech, for example, in his excellent study of the impact of Negro voting,...[1968] has suggested that problems for Black people that are based in the private sector or the economy or are derivative from past discriminatory practices are not only difficult to rectify, but are difficult to raise for public discussion in the first place. Thus, proposals radically to alter the social and economic situation of the Black population are not raised, nor are serious efforts made to alter discrimination in housing or in jobs. In short, many issues that are vitally necessary to the health and well being of Black citizens are often not considered sufficiently compelling or legitimate to reach the public agenda. (pp. 11-12)

This exclusion of issues vital to black interests forced African-Americans to use alternative political forms in the post-World War II era, "including confrontation, disruption, and violence" (Greenberg, Milner, and Olson, 1971, iii). After the passage of the Voting Rights Act in 1965, black people began participating in large numbers in conventional political activities. Conventional politics alone, however, has not allowed African-Americans to overcome the politics of exclusion. Consequently, nonconventional political activity, including popular political movements, became an important vehicle for the expression of black political aspirations.

## Political Movements

Black churches and community organizations, which provide the permanent infrastructure of black political movements, have figured prominently in the successful candidacies of African-Americans. Astute black politicians have long used community, social, and fraternal organizations as reliable means to mobilize black citizens. The mayoral campaigns of Harold Washington (Chicago) and Mel King (Boston) illustrate the importance of community organizations and mass mobilization in conventional political contests (Holli and Green, 1984; Jennings and King, 1986; Bush, 1984). Additionally, Jennings suggests that activists who were associated primarily with nonconventional political activity in the past have begun to participate in conventional electoral contests, bringing with them a third ideological orientation (Jennings, 1990). These "black empowerment activists" challenge the traditional orientations of black politicians in conventional politics. The development of black political leadership through union organizing and labor politics (Widick, 1972) and the successful election campaigns of black candidates considered to be on the political left, like Kenneth Cockrel (Georgakas and Surkin, 1975; Bush, 1984), illustrate this phenomena. Nonconventional politics and popular political movements have been significant in the recruitment and training of black leadership as well as the articulation and dissemination of new political ideas. Political movements further provide important linkages between citizens' interests and organizations.

The theory of comparative advantage is used to explain the different roles and activities that various community groups carry out in political movements and electoral campaigns. Groups like the National Urban League and the NAACP reach their particular clienteles. Political activists target new clientele groups. Black newspapers and radio stations keep the political message alive. Social and fraternal organizations and black churches spread the message, solicit volunteers, and raise funds. Churches in particular have carried out important political functions. They provide arenas wherein groups with different orientations come together to create common goals. Churches act as intermediaries for political parties. Black churches also function as centers for political mobilization, either for specific campaigns or on a continuous basis. Political leaders have historically been recruited and developed from among black clergy. Indeed, black ministers have played varied and significant roles in electoral politics and in programs for economic development.

The direct and indirect political roles that black ministers have carried out include providing access for politicians to their congregations, mobilizing church members for mass protests or elections, and running for political office themselves or acting as power brokers for those who do. The Reverend Jesse Jackson's candidacy for the Democratic Party nomination for president in 1984 and 1988 was one of the most striking new political developments in American politics in recent years (Barker and Walters, 1989). Jackson's bid represented the first time the possibility of an African-American president began to be taken seriously.

Black participation in presidential and local political campaigns has provided interesting information about how to activate the "unmotivated" voter. "Unmotivated" voters are mobilized to participate in politics because of the potential for success of a candidate or cause, and because the process itself encourages the development of a sense of personal empowerment. Group motivation influences black voters as well as individual motivations. Political movements are products of incremental political experiences. Earlier protests have helped people to move from passive to active participation. Scholars note that the policy choices and attitudes of black citizens who do not vote are quite different from those who do, although what these differences are is not clear. An examination of black public opinion provides some clarity on ideological issues.

## Ideological Differences in Black Public Opinion

There has been widespread publicity given to speculation that conservatism has been growing among African-Americans, and especially among those in the middle class, which has grown from approximately 5% in 1955 to 33% in 1985 (Thompson, 1974; Parent and Stekler, 1985; and Farley, 1984). Evidence does not support this speculation, although the presumption that the black middle class is more conservative than the black lower class is understandable. Even though black people share a common experience of oppression, subordination, and discrimination based on race, scholars have noted distinct class differences (McClean, 1984; Johnson and Roark, 1984; Baker, 1964; Frazier, 1939 and 1957; Myrdal, 1944; Drake and Cayton, 1962; Pettigrew, 1964; Moynihan, 1972). While the focus of the distinction was often on sociological traits–such as patterns of consumption, religious values, and voluntary association membership–or on physical traits–such as skin color–researchers noted important political differences as well. For example, an examination of the black elite in 1940 found that 50% of those from the North and almost 80% of those from other regions were still Republican when the party allegiance of the majority of the black masses had shifted to Roosevelt and the Democrats (McBride and Little, 1981; Sites and Mullins, 1985). Class differences were also significant in black support for Marcus Garvey's United Negro Improvement Association in the post-World War I years (Franklin, 1967), and for the Nation of Islam in the 1960s. In our society social class is a key predictor of all sorts of behavior, including political beliefs and actions (Milbrath and Goel, 1977; Thompson, 1974; and Parent and Stekler, 1985; see also occupational distributions of blacks reported in Farley, 1984). What is surprising is that given all the speculation about an increase in black conservatism there is little empirical evidence to document it, though to be sure a few black conservatives have achieved considerable notoriety.

Evidence regarding intrablack attitudinal differences is fragmentary. In national surveys sample populations contain very small numbers of African Americans. For example, a random sample of 1,500 Americans, the standard number surveyed in major opinion polls, contains only 180 African Americans. While such a number is sufficient to say something about black attitudes in general, it is hardly enough to make detailed analyses of differences based on income, education, or other indices of class.

During the past two decades national surveys focused specifically on blacks have occasionally been conducted, such as those done by the Survey Research Center at the University of Michigan in 1984 and the Gallup and Joint Center for Political Studies in 1984. Even so, few reliable studies of black opinion have been published. An examination of published studies yields the following insights. Using the two traditional ways of measuring ideological preference–self-identification and reaction to specific issues–researchers found that few black persons consider themselves to be ideologically conservative (Welch and Foster, 1987). Only 15% of those interviewed in the 1984 Gallup/Joint Center survey placed themselves in the three most conservative positions on a 10-point scale; while 34% placed themselves on the three most liberal positions. On average blacks were 1.2 points more liberal than whites.

Additionally, in reaction to social welfare issues (government spending more money on health, education, welfare, and social issues) black respondents were more liberal than white respondents overall, at all income levels. The liberal gap was greatest among respondents with higher incomes (Gilliam and Whitby, 1987; Parent and Stekler, 1985; Welch and Foster, 1987). On race issues, black citizens were more favorable than white citizens were to busing, affirmative action, and government spending to help African-Americans. There are few studies of black opinion on abortion and school prayer issues. From what is available on black attitudes on these "morality issues," African-Americans are more conservative than white Americans on mandatory school prayer, abortion, and women's rights–except ERA (Secret, Johnson, and Welch, 1986; Seltzer and Smith, 1985; Ransford and Miller, 1983; Granberg and Granberg, 1980; Welch and Combs, 1983, 1985; and Hall and Ferree, 1986). However, blacks are more opposed to the death penalty and more likely to favor gun control than whites (Combs and Comer, 1982; Seltzer and Smith, 1985).

One would expect that a conservative self-identification would be accompanied by advocacy of conservative positions on issues. This is true among whites, although the relationships between identification and activism is not strong. However, a recent study among blacks found that conservative self-identification is almost totally unrelated to conservatism on social welfare spending (Welch and Foster, 1987). Self-declared black conservatives were as likely to take the same liberal positions as black liberals, except on moral issues. Even among highly educated blacks, self-identification and issue-position are not related.

Like other Americans, it appears that blacks became slightly more conservative during the 1970s and early 1980s (Welch and Combs, 1983, 1985; Gilliam and Whitby, 1987). However, blacks moved less far to the right than did whites, especially the white upper classes. There is little solid data on the extent of the black shift to the right during this period for two reasons: a lack of comparability of samples over time;

and, where such samples are available, a lack of sufficient numbers of black respondents to make reliable estimates.

On social welfare issues, Welch and Combs (1983, 1985) found few differences among African-Americans of different social classes among the small numbers of black people sampled in several National Opinion Research Center (NORC) General Social Surveys. Middle-class blacks were less likely than lower-class blacks to support federal welfare programs, but they were more liberal in supporting federal programs for health and education. Seltzer and Smith (1985) present similar findings from the 1982 NORC data, using education as an indication of social status (cf. Caldwell, 1978). Parent and Stekler (1985), who used small samples of blacks from the Survey Research Center's National Election Studies, also found middle-class blacks less likely than other blacks to support federal guarantees for jobs and standards of living. Additionally, Gilliam and Whitby (1987) also found the black middle class slightly more conservative than the lower class on the use of public spending to solve a variety of social and economic problems. Using a much larger sample (over 1,000 blacks and 1,400 whites) from the Joint Center/Gallup 1984 election polls, Welch and Foster (1987) found that blacks of higher income are less enthusiastic about social welfare spending than lower-income blacks. The class differences, however, were less than those among whites. Gilliam and Whitby (1987) also found class differences considerably less pronounced among blacks than among whites.

What is clear from available though fragmentary data is that patterns of public opinion among African-Americans do not fit easily into the traditional typologies used to explain patterns of white American public opinion. Although the black middle class is somewhat more conservative than the black lower classes, when considered in terms of income group overall, blacks are substantially more liberal than whites. The black middle class is more liberal relative to the white middle class than is the black lower class to the white lower class. The class differences among African-Americans are much smaller than in the white community. When comparing intraracial ideological patterns it appears that members of the black middle class are somewhat more conservative on social welfare issues than black citizens with lower SES, but less conservative on race and morality issues.

Parent and Stekler (1985) show that middle-class blacks are more likely than lower-class blacks to assert that civil rights progress is too slow, and less likely to agree that there has been a lot of change in civil rights. They are also more likely than lower-class blacks to say they identify closely with other blacks. On the other hand, Bolce and Gray (1979), in interviews with 600 New York City residents, discovered that lower-class blacks were more supportive of affirmative action than were higher status blacks.

Others have found few consistent class differences in support of race issues (Welch and Foster, 1987). The safest generalization to make concerning class differences in the black community regarding civil rights and race issues is that there is no clearcut difference in attitudes. Such a conclusion is not surprising given that on issues of racial and legal subordination blacks have historically been treated as if class did not matter.

On moral issues intraracial differences have been examined less frequently but, as in attitudes toward racial issues, there is certainly no evidence that the black middle class is more conservative than the lower class (Welch and Foster, 1987; Seltzer and Smith, 1985). On certain issues, such as abortion, sex education, drug education, homosexuality, and birth control, the black middle class is probably more liberal than their lower-income and less-educated peer group (Seltzer and Smith, 1985; Hall and Ferree, 1986). On the other hand, middle-class blacks, especially men, are more conservative in their attitudes toward the roles of women than are other blacks (Ransford and Miller, 1983).

In terms of gender, black women are more likely to vote Democratic than black men (Bolce, 1985). One study examining four general issues (social welfare, military spending, traditional moral values, and affirmative action) found that while women were more opposed to military spending, there were no significant sex differences on the other issues (Welch and Foster, 1987). One study of attitudes toward support for a woman for president found black women more supportive than black men (Sigelman and Welch, 1984).

In conclusion, there is not much evidence of a new black conservatism. Furthermore, on issues other than social welfare, there is no evidence whatsoever that the black middle class is more conservative than the black lower class. Indeed, on many race and morality issues, the middle class is more liberal. In the overall spectrum of American politics, middle-class blacks are quite liberal.

## Political Exclusion, Political Power, and Black Politics

The political relationship of African-Americans to the U.S. political community for most of the last 400 years has been one of powerlessness. This fundamental political relationship took variant forms in 1865 and in 1877 and during the Great Migration to the urban North and West from 1894 to 1914, but did not change. Social and economic issues important to black citizens could not be placed on the public policy agenda because of the structure of racial politics, specifically disfranchisement and dilution.

Politically almost completely subordinated in the South, African-Americans at the turn of the century turned to the accommodationist politics of Booker T. Washington (Katznelson, 1976; Holden, 1973). By 1915, however, even Washington supporters were disillusioned by the response of the Republican party to black aspirations. New organizations, including the NAACP, pioneered different strategies to advance black interests. The ways in which black citizens were linked to the polity in northern cities during the machine era provided participation without representation and power. Black political activities were controlled and directed by the bosses of urban political machines (Katznelson, 1976; 1981). Progressive politics and the New Deal brought reform to local and national governmental structures. With regard to African-American citizens, however, the changes were largely symbolic; there was no substantial inclusion in the political process (Fainstein and Fainstein, 1974; Harrigan, 1985). Improvements that did occur in black life during the New Deal were largely linked to the general improvements experienced by all Americans because of the policies of FDR's administration. And in many locales, relief was still distributed in a segregated and discriminatory manner (Mayor LaGuardia, 1969).

A. Philip Randolph's "March on Washington" movements in 1941 and 1942 began the active phase of the modern civil rights movement. The creation of the Federal Employment Practices Commission, the desegregation of war industries, and in 1949 the desegregation of the armed forces were all consequences of an emerging mass movement. The Supreme Court decision in *Brown* (1954) and the victories in the Montgomery bus boycott (1955-56) were historical catalysts for the explosive direct-action campaigns that accelerated in the late 1950s, and for the student movement in the early 1960s. These sociopolitical movements confronted and challenged the nation's century-old practices and laws promoting racial and political subordination of African-Americans.

The modern civil rights movement (since 1940) began as an attempt to improve black life by seeking a more just society (the "beloved community," see Carson, 1981; McAdam, 1988). The objectives of the movement were as much philosophical, religious, moral, and social as they were political. Moral appeals often elicited moral responses from Americans as individuals and from private groups. But the pragmatic realities of the American political and decision-making structure resulted in very slow change in government policy (Miroff, 1979). The apparent reluctance of the federal government to protect the constitutional rights of black citizens led to disillusionment among many activists.

Some sectors of the civil rights movement became politicized and radicalized. Politics was viewed as the best hope for getting black concerns onto public policy agendas. Countervailing power was viewed as the best means to protect black life and interests. Those who took the political promises of the American creed to heart—like the members of the Mississippi Freedom Democratic Party in 1964–did not realize the constraints inherent in the American political system. Others–equating the status of black Americans with that of colonized peoples around the globe–advocated far-reaching changes in the American political system. For those who pursued power within conventional politics, the built-in limits to what could be accomplished in the public arena meant that even after the transition to black rule in many jurisdictions, black empowerment remained illusive.

Until 1965 the basic thrust of black political efforts was a search for power, i.e., a struggle to influence the authoritative decisions that affected black lives. In legislation, litigation, coalitions, accommodation, and confrontation, in demonstrations and mobilizations of public opinion, the goal was always power and influence. Disfranchisement, dilution, and the structure of racial politics were the major barriers to the acquisition of power. Politics, conventional and nonconventional, were viewed as a means to overcome this politics of exclusion. Structural barriers to black political participation were lowered though not eliminated by the Voting Rights Act (1965) and decisions in *Gomillion* (1960) and other dilution cases (Bell, 1980). However, even after dramatic increases in black participation, along with success in electoral and conventional politics, the search for power continues. The most salient question is why.

There are three major reasons why the search for power is far from over: the limits and constraints of our constitutional government (e.g., federalism and the Dillon rule); political change in the structures of urban and national government; and the overall structure of power in America. Public power in the United States is fragmented and dispersed at the national level into separate institutions–none of which can make and implement policy without the positive action of others. This fragmentation and dispersal of public policy-making authority necessitates deal making, compromise, and incrementalism. The function of these devices has been to make it difficult for any elected faction to gain a majority and directly exercise popular will. The fear was not the tyranny of the despot–but the tyranny of the crowd (Parenti, 1983; Greenberg, 1986).

Additionally, federalism grants power to both the national and state governments. One example of the consequences of this system was the decision of the state of Mississippi in the Neshoba County murders (Bell, 1980, pp. 216-218) not to prosecute the defendants for the murders of three civil rights workers–James E. Chaney, Andrew Goodwin, and Michael H. Schwerner. The only legal recourse available when the state declined to bring criminal charges against local sheriffs and 15 other assailants was for the federal government to charge the assailants with the violation of the victims' civil rights. In this case, the federal structure did not give jurisdiction to the national government to indict those convicted under the civil rights statutes for murder.

The Dillon rule made the autonomy and existence of cities and towns dependent on state legislatures (Goodall and Sprengel, 1975).[5] While states do grant home-rule charters that increase the autonomy of large cities and municipalities, these charters can be changed or revoked at any time. Thus in Detroit and Atlanta when African-American mayors were first elected the city charters were changed to limit each mayors' tenure to two terms.[6]

Changes in urban and national political structures also contributed to the politics of exclusion. From about 1900 to the early 1930s (later in some jurisdictions, like Chicago) urban political machines, geographically based in white ethnic communities, dominated urban political life in northern cities. These machines were able to provide their ethnic constituencies with material rewards in exchange for solid political support at the polls. There is considerable debate over whether ethnic political machines provided anything more than symbolic political rewards or whether the ability of ethnic political bosses to broker for the substantive interest of their constituencies was coopted by more powerful political and economic elites (Katznelson, 1981). Also at issue is whether assimilation theories about white ethnics using political machines to promote social and economic mobility have much foundation in fact (Parenti, 1970a). It is suggested that what brought about upward mobility for ethnic immigrants was the same thing that assisted everyone else: the New Deal and the improvement in the general standard of living for other white Americans brought about by an expanding economy (Hamilton, 1982; Parenti, 1970a).

Whether assimilation theories are accurate or not, the structures of urban politics did allow political machines controlled by white ethnics to provide jobs, social welfare benefits, and business opportunities primarily if not exclusively to their ethnic constituencies. Eventually these structures were changed by progressive reform movements so that the opportunity to use public power to serve particular constituencies no longer existed when the transition to black rule occurred in the seventies. For example, for Curley's administration in Boston and for the bosses of Tammany Hall, lawsuits to stop preferential hiring of members of the Irish community were never a serious threat. For black mayors, however, from Birmingham to Detroit to Richmond, lawsuits challenging the provision of jobs and city contracts for black citizens are relatively commonplace.

Progressive reform not only changed the structures of urban politics, it also changed the patterns of bias within these structures. The new patterns disadvantaged African-Americans in the political process while they advantaged new groups. The progressive movement introduced new values into the political culture that make it difficult for black administrations to provide substantive as well as symbolic rewards to black constituencies. In addition, reform changed the ways in which poor and unorganized citizens were linked to the polity, resulting in demobilization and depoliticization of the poor in the cities.

Even the basic ethos of the political system changed under reform governments, from a politics of power to one of efficiency (Grimshaw, 1984). Public bureaucracies replaced machines for the distribution of social welfare benefits. Unlike political machines, the bureaucracies were not even symbolically accountable and responsive to their clientele. Unorganized citizens, especially the poor, were no longer linked to the polity through political parties and city hall—a system that, despite its flaws, did provide poor ethnic citizens with some measure of political currency: their vote. Now poor citizens were linked to the polity through bureaucratic agencies, with quasi-governmental power insulated from popular control (Harrigan, 1985). One consequence of this was that by the 1960s and 1970s urban political movements developed among Hispanic and African-American populations who sought popular control of public bureaucracies, i.e., community control of schools, welfare agencies, public health-care providers, and the police (Fainstein and Fainstein, 1974).

Progressive reform effectively discredited the private-regarding ethos of "to the victory goes the spoils" which dominated political culture during the era of political "machines." In its place a public-regarding ethos evolved, according to which the use of public resources for private gain could only be legitimized in terms of the general public good (Harrigan, 1985). Predominately upper-class Protestant reformers, supported by other groups, sought to break the power of the predominately lower-class

Catholic political bosses in the name of "good government." Changes in political structure were to put an end to widespread graft and corruption. Historians remind us, however, that whatever else the progressive reform movement did, it did not eliminate corruption from the urban political landscape. Progressive reform may have simply replaced the ethnic political machine with a new kind of machine, one which symbolically served black interests better, but which left black citizens as unrepresented, excluded, and manipulated as before (Fainstein and Fainstein, 1974; Harrigan, 1985). The politics of exclusion has thus worked to the detriment of black political interests in the North and West as well as the South. Even so, disfranchisement in the South became the primary target of efforts to end second-class citizenship in American political life.

The focus of much of the political activity among African-Americans since 1940 has been on getting the right to participate on an equal basis. This is what Hamilton (1986) refers to as a politics of rights. As black political participation increased and the structures of racial politics changed, assessments began to be made of the limits and potential of political activity for addressing social and economic ills (Preston, Henderson, Jr., and Puryear, 1982). The politics of rights was supplanted by a politics of resources (Hamilton, 1986). The salient concern shifted from participating in the political system to the terms of that participation and to the likely consequences of that participation.

One of the most important contemporary issues is the degree to which black political activity can lead to improvements in the economic and social status of African-Americans. What are the limits and potential of political participation for achieving black aspirations; what are the strategic and policy implications of contemporary political evolution; and, what are the directions and future possibilities for political action. The question Martin Luther King, Jr., raised in 1968 remains a critical one today: where do we go from here (King, 1968)?

It has only been since the late sixties that the third obstacle to the attainment of political influence and effective representation for black citizens–the way in which power is structured–has received some attention. Political violence and political movements in the North and West, where African-Americans had not been excluded from the franchise, brought into sharp relief the necessity for continuing the struggle for political power. The transformation of protest into politics did yield victories in local political contests. But the initial euphoria generated by the capture of city hall eventually gave way to more sober assessments of the limits of of public power.

Explanations for the limitations of conventional politics generally focus on the built-in constraints on public policy-making (Hamilton, 1982; Greenberg, Milner, and Olson, 1971; Katznelson and Kesselman, 1987). The ideology of democratic liberalism, it is reasoned, removes certain issues from the legitimate realm of public discussion. Because government is limited in a constitutional system, certain issues are considered "private," and as such are beyond the scope of public decision makers. One of these issues, it is argued, is the use of public political resources to enhance economic position or to stimulate social mobility (Jaynes and Williams, Jr., 1989). Not only does such an explanation contradict widely accepted definitions for politics–the authoritative allocation of value (Easton, 1971), or decisions about who gets what, when, and how (Lasswell, 1958)–it also ignores the fact that much contemporary and historical policy-making calls into question this concept of limits (Greenberg, 1986; Harris, 1986; Dolbeare and Edelman, 1981).

A number of examples raise significant questions about the notion that it is unacceptable in our system of government to use politics to enhance economic or allocational status. General policies as well as government largess given to specific economic actors dramatically contradict assumptions about the limits of political decision making on economic allocation.[7] There has been only minor public outcry about spending between $150 and $200 billion of taxpayers dollars to bail out failed savings and loans (S & Ls) institutions. On the contrary, the S & L bailout, as with other uses of public resources in the private sector, is considered to be a legitimate use of public power to impact private economic activity.

The issue then is not *whether* public power should be used to enhance private allocational status, but *for whom*. Therefore, conventional political analysts are not necessarily mistaken when they claim that the conventional limits of politics in our system make it difficult to use politics to alter the allocational status of black Americans. Rather, a broader analytical perspective is required to explain this apparent contradiction. A broader perspective indicates that for some groups in the polity (elites) the use of public power to support economic status is considered legitimate. For other groups (nonelites) the use of public power to support economic status is not considered legitimate, except perhaps in a period of crisis. How are these differential sets of rules justified? And how does the existence of differential rules in the polity impact black political aspirations? These questions direct attention to the third obstacle to the attainment of political power for African-Americans: the way in which power is structured in the United States.

Scholars debate the comparative merits of a number of competing theories and models of American politics (Dye, 1979; Parenti, 1970b, 1983; Greenberg, 1986; Katznelson and Kesselman, 1987; Hawley and Wirt, 1968; Dolbeare and Edelman, 1981; Dahl, 1961; Hunter, 1953; Mills, 1956; Connolly, 1967; Mayo, 1960; Polsby, 1963; Lindblom, 1977; and Bachrach and Baratz, 1962). This debate is not esoteric in terms of black political interests. A review of this debate indicates that power is organized both privately and publicly in the United States. There are important structures of mediation between the two. Thus, public officials do not simply carry out the formal role expectations of their positions; rather they act as brokers between public policy and private power.

The traditional concept of American politics as a constitutional system with clearly defined constraints on public power and policy making limits discussion to the arena of public power and politics. The context and limits of the public exercise of power, however, are influenced to varying degrees by the structure and organization of private power. One way this private organization of power influences decision making is through the power of nondecisions (Bachrach and Baratz, 1962)–that is the power to set the public agenda. When policy makers and politicians try to move outside the "acceptable" ranges of public life they encounter enormous resistance and oftentimes defeat of their proposals. Some major aspects of life in the U.S., such as the rights of private ownership or the presence and persistence of economic inequality, never receive the attention and debate that they deserve (Domhoff, 1978). Candidates for political office do not build them into their campaigns, nor do elected and appointed officials raise them in legislative chambers. Thus, merely electing black candidates to public office does not ensure that issues of concern to African-Americans, such as economic inequality between racial groups, will receive appropriate attention in the public policy-making process. Any comprehensive reading of black political life in America has to confront the implications of the public/private dimensions of power.

There are inherent limits, then, on the exercise of power within the political system. The fragmentation and dispersal of power and policy making through federalism, separation-of-powers, and other constitutional provisions does not invalidate the power elite thesis. The structure of private power may be conceptualized in many ways–as monolithic and hierarchical, as pluralistic, as institutionally-based, as oligarchical, as plutocratic–and in all its forms private power influences public decision-making. This influence is not normally directly exercised through the state (i.e., national, state, or local governmental structures). Rather, private power is exercised through mediating structures, some examples of which include political parties, political campaigns, lobbying, think tanks, the media, the educational system, policy formulation, and the law.

The contemporary challenge for black politics goes beyond the capture of elective office, participation in conventional political arenas, and placing the concerns of black citizens on public agendas. The larger challenge concerns effective representation of black interests in all the significant arenas of policy formulation: elite and nonelite, public and private. Effective representation[8] requires substantive inclusion of African-Americans in all areas of political life. It is the political inclusion of African-Americans that alone holds out the promise of transforming American politics, of bringing about effective representation for all Americans within the body politic.

Historically, political change has occurred in the United States in evolutionary ways. Changes in political structure were accompanied by changes in the patterns of bias within the system (Harrigan, 1985). These patterns of bias automatically advantage some in the political system while automatically disadvantaging others. There is a need to identify the patterns of bias that operate at various levels of American politics to limit black aspirations. There is also a need to stimulate and legitimize public debate of options for political change that could move us from a politics of exclusion to one of inclusion.

A politics of inclusion is concerned with more than the effective representation of black interests in the political system. For example, the political movements of the sixties generally sought black empowerment in a context of the creation of a just society. The nation was called upon to live up to the highest ideals of the American creed. Indeed, central to Myrdal's thesis of the "American Dilemma" was the contradiction between the espoused ideals and the historical practices of white Americans, especially with regard to issues of race (Myrdal, 1944).

A politics of inclusion resurrects the moral dimension of American politics. The demand for effective representation of all citizens moves us toward the ideal of a just society in the true sense of democracy—one in which political liberty exists because all citizens not only have the right to vote, but also have an equal chance to influence effectively the decisions that affect their lives.

## Summary

An evaluation of the participation of African-Americans in the political life of the nation since the 1940s indicates a tremendous upsurge in voter registration and turnout, especially in the aftermath of the passage of the Voting Rights Act of 1965. In presidential elections, the gap narrowed between participation rates of blacks and whites. Increased participation meant that elected officials became more sensitive to black needs when the interests of African-Americans and Euro-Americans converged. However, old problems remain and new issues emerge as the limits of political participation become more evident. These new issues include how to manage ethnic and racial group relations, how to manage interracial conflict, and how to keep black elected officials accountable to their constituencies.

As long as the politics of exclusion is operative in American politics both conventional and nonconventional alternatives of political participation will be important for African-Americans. Conventional politics continue to be significant not only because of access to public power centers and policy making, but also because of the brokerage factor as well as the political, educational, and symbolic functions that officeholders carry out in the public and private arenas of power. Concomitantly, nonconventional politics will continue to be an important avenue for mobilizing black political aspirations as long as the politics of exclusion mitigate against effective political participation in the polity.

The political behavior of African-Americans in the period 1940 to the present is best understood as a search for power in both conventional and nonconventional political terms. The goal has not only been to gain full participation in the public political arena, but to achieve effective political representation throughout the polity. The struggle for a politics of inclusion, which focused during the civil rights movement on gaining access to conventional political processes, continues as a search for the ways and means to achieve full participation in all political arenas of the polity.

# Appendix A

A typology of group-polity, group-leadership relationships can be constructed using the three dimensions–descriptive representativeness, responsiveness (substantive representation), and efficacy (actual representation)–yielding eight possible ideal-types:

## Table 3-6

Typology of Group-Polity Relationship and Internal Group Structure

|  | Representative | | Not Representative | |
|---|---|---|---|---|
|  | Responsive | Not Responsive | Responsive | Not Responsive |
| Efficacious | 1. Clear democracy | 2. Detached oligarchy | 5. Paternalism | 6. Efficacious autocracy |
| Not efficacious | 3. Ineffectual democracy | 4. Apparent democracy | 7. Ineffectual paternalism | 8. Clear tyranny |

1. The policy or the group's leadership is descriptively representative, responsive, and efficacious. We may call this case *clear democracy*.

2. The polity or the group's leadership is descriptively representative and efficacious, but is unresponsive to group needs. Here the forms of democracy are intact and are seen to be operating, but the group's participating leadership elite has been co-opted or bought off so that while it participates in the larger political system, it no longer speaks for those it claims to represent. We may call this case *detached oligarchy*.

3. The polity or the group's leadership is descriptively representative, responsive, but ineffectual. We may call this case *ineffectual democracy*.

4. In this fairly unlikely case, the polity or the group's leadership, though descriptively representative, is both unresponsive and ineffectual. The polity or group leadership's unresponsiveness is masked by its lack of effectiveness. We may, therefore, call this case *apparent democracy*.

5. The polity or the group's leadership is responsive though not descriptively representative, but is efficacious in promoting its goals. We may call this case *paternalism*.

6. The polity or the group's leadership is neither descriptively representative nor responsive, but promotes its goals effectively. We may call this case *efficacious autocracy*.

7. The polity or the group's leadership, though ineffectual and not descriptively representative does try to be responsive. We may call this case *ineffectual paternalism*.

8. The polity or the group's leadership is not descriptively responsive, nor is it responsive or effectual. We may call this case *clear tyranny*.

Utilizing this typology, we can ask, cross-nationally, if racial group relationships are characterized by high or low descriptive representation, responsiveness, and efficacy; in what combination; and with what consequences.

## Notes

1. Examples include lynchings, nightriders, murders, burnings, mob violence, physical assaults, and economic deprivations, i.e., losing a job, denial of loans, etc.

2. The white primary was the process (legal until 1944) of excluding blacks from the Democratic party and thereby precluding blacks from voting in the Democratic primaries. This was the most effective mechanism used to disenfranchise blacks throughout the South.

3. The concepts of "critical" and "routine" are used by Katznelson to define critical and routine periods in the history of racial politics. He writes: "In social terms, the student of race politics can distinguish between critical and routine historical periods, the former being the periods when critical structural political decisions were made institutionalizing power differentials between racial groups... Since 'organization is the mobilization of bias,' ... [Schattschneider, 1960] structure not only limits but also shapes the direction of choice. With Apter 'the structure may be defined as the relationships in a social situation which limit the choice process to a particular range of alternative,' while 'the behavioral may be defined as the selection process in choice, i.e., deciding between alternatives.' ... [Apter and Eckstein, 1963] Utilizing this distinction, critical decisions are structural, routine decisions behavioral ... [McFarland, 1969]." (Katznelson, 1976)

4. This issue is discussed more fully in the last section of this chapter, "Political Exclusion, Political Power, and Black Politics."

5. Judge J.F. Dillon, in the 1860s, in what became known as Dillon's Rule, established the interpretation of local powers that makes local governments creations that exist at the pleasure of the state. The state can alter their structure or even abolish them (Goodall and Sprengel, 1975, p. 38).

6. Coleman Young was able to have this provision changed; Maynard Jackson was not. Jackson had to wait out the mayoralty of Andy Young before running again successfully for his third term.

7. Tax abatements, price supports, favorable tax policies aimed at specific industries or corporations, the use of governmental power to negotiate favorable trade policies, and progrowth urban renewal policies are examples of general policies. The use of Urban Development Action Grant monies in Rhode Island to refurbish a hotel lobby, the use of PIC monies to pay a California agribusiness not to plant rice in a lake, and the Chrysler bailout are all examples of transfer payments to specific companies.

8. See Katznelson (1976, pp. 26-28) for a discussion of the meaning of effective and efficacious representation within the context of the structure of racial politics. Also see Appendix A for his typology of group-polity relations and internal group structure.

# References

Alford, R.R. & Friedland, R. (1975). Political Participation and Public Policy. In A. Inkeles, J. Coleman, and N. Smelser (Eds.), *Annual Review of Sociology, 1*. Palo Alto: Annual Reviews Inc.

Altshuler, A.A. (1970). *Community Control: The Black Demand for Participation in Large American Cities*. New York: Pegasus.

Bachrach, P. & Baratz, M.S. (1962). The Two Faces of Power. *American Political Science Review, 56*, 547-552.

Bachrach, P. & Baratz, M.S. (1970). *Power and Poverty*. New York: Oxford University Press.

Baker, R.S. (1964). *Following the Color Line: American Negro Citizenship in the Progressive Era*. New York: Harper and Row. (Original edition published in 1908).

Barker, L., & Walters, R.W. (Eds.). (1989). *Jesse Jackson's 1984 Presidential Campaign: Challenge and Change in American Politics*. Urbana, IL: University of Illinois Press.

Bass, J. & DeVries, W. (1976). *The Transformation of Southern Politics*. New York: Basic Books.

Bell, D.A., Jr. (1980). *Race, Racism, and American Law* (2d ed.). Boston: Little Brown.

Black, E. (1976). *Southern Governors and Civil Rights*. Cambridge, MA: Harvard University Press.

Boamah-Wiafe, D. (1990). *The Black Experience in Contemporary America*. Omaha, NE: Wisdom Publications.

Bolce, L.H. (1985). Reagan and the Reverse Gender Gap. *Public Opinion Quarterly, 15*, 372-385.

Bolce, L. & Gray, S.H. (1979). Blacks, Whites, and Race Politics. *Public Interest, 53*, 61-75.

Breitman, G. (1967). *The Last Year of Malcolm X: The Evolution of a Revolutionary*. New York: Pathfinder Press.

*Brown v. Board of Education*, 347 U.S. 483 (1954).

Brown, H.R. (1969). *Die Nigger Die*. New York: Dial Press.

Bush, R. (Ed.). (1984). *The New Black Vote.* San Francisco: Synthesis Publications.

Button, J.W. (1978). *Black Violence.* Princeton, NJ: Princeton University Press.

Caldwell, E. (1978). The Rising Status of Commitment. *Black Enterprise, 9,* 38-42.

Campbell, D. & Feagin, J.R. (1975). Black Politics in the South. *Journal of Politics, 37,* 129-162.

Carmichael, S. & Hamilton, C.V. (1967). *Black Power.* New York: Random House.

Carson, C. (1981). *In Struggle: SNCC and the Black Awakening of the 1960s.* Cambridge, MA: Harvard University Press.

Cassel, C. (1979). Changes in Electoral Participation in the South. *Journal of Politics, 41,* 907-917.

Combs, M. & Comer, J. (1982). Race and Capital Punishment: A Longitudinal Analysis. *Phylon, 43,* 350-359.

Connolly, W. (1967). *Political Science and Ideology.* New York: Atherton Press.

Coombs, D., Alsikafi, M.H., Bryan, C.H., & Webber, I. (1977). Black Political Control in Greene County, Alabama. *Rural Sociology, 42,* 398-406.

Dahl, R.A. (1961). *Who Governs?* New Haven, CT: Yale University Press.

Danigelis, N. (1978). Black Political Participation in the United States. *American Sociological Review, 43,* 756-771.

Davidson, C. (1984). Minority Vote Dilution. In C. Davidson (Ed.), *Minority Vote Dilution.* Washington, DC: Howard University Press.

Davidson, C. & Korbel, G. (1981). At-Large Elections and Minority Group Representation. *Journal of Politics, 43,* 982-1005.

Dolbeare, K.M. & Edelman, M.J. (1981). *American Politics* (4th ed.). Lexington, MA: D. C. Heath.

Domhoff, G.W. (1978). *The Powers That Be.* New York: Vintage.

Drake, S.C. & Cayton, R.C. (1962). *Black Metropolis.* New York: Harper and Row. (Original edition published in 1945).

Dye, T.K. (1979). *Who's Running America? The Carter Years* (2d ed.). Englewood Cliffs, NJ: Prentice-Hall.

Easton, D. (1971). *The Political System: An Inquiry into the State of Political Science* (2d ed.). New York: Knopf.

Eisinger, P.K. (1980). *The Politics of Displacement: Racial and Ethnic Transition in Three American Cities.* New York: Academic Press.

Eisinger, P.K. (1983). *Black Employment in City Government, 1973-1980* Washington, DC: Joint Center for Political Studies.

Fainstein, N.I. & Fainstein, S.S. (1974). *Urban Political Movements: The Search for Power by Minority Groups in American Cities.* Englewood Cliffs, NJ: Prentice-Hall.

Farley, R. (1984). *Black and Whites.* Cambridge, MA: Harvard University Press.

Feagin, J.R. (1972). Civil Rights Voting by Southern Congressman. *Journal of Politics, 34,* 484-499.

Franklin, J.H. (1967). *From Slavery to Freedom.* New York: Knopf.

Frazier, E.F. (1939). *The Negro Family in the United States.* Chicago: University of Chicago Press.

Frazier, E.F. (1957). *Black Bourgeoise: The Rise of a New Middle Class in the United States.* Glencoe, IL: Free Press.

Georgakas, D. & Surkin, M. (1975). *Detroit: I Do Mind Dying.* New York: St. Martin's Press.

Gilliam, F. & Whitby, K.J. (1987). Race, Class and Abortion Attitudes: An Ethclass Model. Paper presented at the annual meeting of the Midwest Political Science Association, April, 1987, Chicago, Illinois.

Glantz, O. (1960). The Negro Voter in Northern Industrial Cities. *Western Political Quarterly, 13,* 999-1010.

Goodall, L.E. & Sprengel, D.P. (1975). *The American Metropolis* (2d ed.). Columbus, OH: Charles E. Merrill.

Granberg, D. & Granberg, B. (1980). Abortion Attitudes, 1965-1980: Trends and Determinants. *Family Planning Perspectives, 12,* 250-261.

Greeley, A. (1971). *Why Can't They Be Like Us.* New York: E. P. Dutton.

Greenberg, E.S. (1986). *The American Political System: A Radical Approach* (4th ed.). Boston: Little Brown.

Greenberg, E.S., Milner, N., & Olson, D.J. (1971). *Black Politics: The Inevitability of Conflict/Readings.* New York: Holt, Rinehart, and Winston.

Greer, E.S. (1979). *Big Steel.* New York: Monthly Review Press.

Grimshaw, W. (1984). Is Chicago Ready for Reform? Or, A New Agenda for Harold Washington. In M.G. Holli and P.M. Green (Eds.). *The Making of the Mayor: Chicago 1983.* Grand Rapids, MI: Eerdmans.

Hall, E.J. & Ferree, M.M. (1986). Race Differences in Abortion Attitudes. *Public Opinion Quarterly, 50,* 193-207.

Hamilton, C.V. (1982). Foreword. In M. B. Preston, L. J. Henderson, Jr., and P. Puryear (Eds.), *The New Black Politics: The Search for Power.* New York: Longman.

Hamilton, C.V. (1986). Social Policy and the Welfare of Black Americans: From Rights to Resources. *Political Science Quarterly, 101* (2), 239-255.

Harrigan, J.J. (1985). *Political Change in the Metropolis* (3d ed.). Boston: Little Brown.

Harris, F.R. (1986). *America's Democracy: The Ideal and the Reality* (3d ed.). Glenview, IL: Scott, Foresman.

Hawley, W.D. & Wirt, F.M. (Eds.). (1968). *The Search for Community Power*. Englewood Cliffs, NJ: Prentice-Hall.

Herbers, J. (1965, February 2). Dr. King and 770 Others Seized in Alabama Protest. *New York Times*, p. 1.

Holden, M. (1973). *The Politics of the Black "Nation."* New York: Chandler.

Holli, M.G. & Green, P.M. (Eds.) (1984). *The Making of the Mayor: Chicago 1983*. Grand Rapids, MI: Eerdsmans.

Hunter, D.H. (1974). *Federal Review of Voting Changes*. Washington, DC: Joint Center for Political Studies.

Hunter, F. (1953). *Community Power Structure*. Chapel Hill, NC: University of North Carolina Press.

James, M. (1973). *The People's Lawyers*. New York: Holt, Rinehart and Winston.

Jaynes, G.D. & Williams, R.M., Jr. (Eds.). (1989). *A Common Destiny: Blacks and American Society*. Washington, DC: National Academy Press.

Jennings, J. (1990). *The Politics of Black Empowerment: The Transformation of Black Activism in Urban America*. Detroit: Wayne State University Press.

Jennings, J. & King, M. (1986). *From Access to Power: Black Politics in Boston*. Cambridge, MA: Schenkman Books.

Johnson, M. & Roark, J.L. (1984). *Black Masters: A Free Family of Color in the Old South*. New York: W.W. Norton.

Jones, M. (1972). Black Officeholders in Local Governments in the South. Paper presented at the 68th annual meeting of the American Political Science Association, Los Angeles.

Karnig, A. & Welch, S. (1980). *Black Representation and Urban Policy*. Chicago: University of Chicago Press.

Katznelson, I. (1976). *Black Men, White Cities: Race, Politics, and Migration in the United States, 1900-30, and Britain, 1948-68*. Chicago: University of Chicago Press.

Katznelson, I. (1981). *City Trenches: Urban Politics and the Patterning of Class in the United* (2d ed.). Chicago: University of Chicago Press.

Katznelson, I. & Kesselman, M. (1987). *The Politics of Power: A Critical Introduction to American Government* (3rd ed.). San Diego: Harcourt Brace Jovanovich.

Keech, W.R. (1968). *The Impact of Negro Voting*. Chicago: Rand McNally.

Kernell, S. (1973). Comment: A Re-evaluation of Black Voting in Mississippi. *American Political Science Review, 67*, 1307-1318.

King, M.L., Jr. (1968). *Where Do We Go From Here?: Chaos or Community.* Boston: Beacon Press.

Lasswell, H. (1958). *Politics: Who Gets What, When, How.* Cleveland: Meridian Books.

Levy, M.R. & Kramer, M.S. (1972). *The Ethnic Factor.* New York: Simon and Schuster.

Lindblom, C. (1977). *Politics and Markets.* New York: Basic Books.

Lipset, S.M. (1963). *Political Man: The Social Bases of Politics.* New York: Doubleday.

Lipsky, M. (1980). *Street-Level Bureaucracy: Dilemmas of the Individual in Public Services.* New York: Russell Sage Foundation.

Marshall, D. & Tabb, D. (1985). *Minority Participation and Political Payoffs in California.* New York: Basic Books.

Mayo, H. (1960). *An Introduction to Democratic Theory.* New York: Oxford University Press.

Mayor LaGuardia's Commission on the Harlem Riot. (1969). *The Complete Report of Mayor LaGuardia's Commission on the Harlem Riot of March 19, 1935.* New York: Arno Press.

McAdam, D. (1982). *Political Process and the Development of Black Insurgency.* Chicago: University of Chicago Press.

McAdam, D. (1988). *Freedom Summer,* New York: Oxford University Press.

McBride, D. & Little, M. (1981). The Afro-American Elite, 1930-1940. *Phylon, 42,* 105-119.

McClean, V. (1984). Historical Examples of Black Conservatism. *Western Journal of Black Studies, 8,* 148-153.

Meier, A. (Ed.). (1970). *The Transformation of Activism.* Chicago: Aldine Publishing.

Milbrath, L. & Goel, M. (1977). *Political Participation* (2d ed.). Chicago: Rand McNally.

Mills, C.W. (1956). *The Power Elite.* New York: Oxford University Press.

Miroff, B. (1979). *Pragmatic Illusions: The Presidential Politics of John F. Kennedy.* New York: Longman.

Morris, A. (1984). *The Origins of the Civil Rights Movements: Black Communities Organizing for Change.* New York: Free Press.

Moss, L.E. (1977). *Black Political Ascendancy in Urban Centers and Black Control of the Local Police Function: An Exploratory Analysis.* San Francisco: R & E Associates.

Moynihan, D.P. (1972). The Schism in Black America. *Public Interest, 27,* 3-24.

Myrdal, G. (1944). *An American Dilemma: The Negro Problem and Modern Democracy.* New York: Harper and Row.

Neiburg, H. L. (1969). *Political Violence.* New York: St. Martin's Press.

Olsen, M. (1970). Social and Political Participation of Blacks. *American Sociological Review, 35*, 682-697.

Parent, W. & Stekler, P. (1985). The Political Implications of Economic Stratification in the Black Community. *Western Political Quarterly, 38*, 521-537.

Parenti, M. (1970a). Assimilation and Counter-Assimilation: From Civil Rights to Black Radicalism. In P. Green, and S. Levinson (Eds.), *Power and Community: Dissenting Essays in Political Science.* New York: Vintage.

Parenti, M. (1970b). Power and Pluralism: A View From the Bottom. *Journal of Politics, 32*, 501-530.

Parenti, M. (1983). *Democracy for the Few* (4th ed.). New York: St. Martin's Press.

Parker, F.R. (1984). Racial Gerrymandering and Legislative Reapportionment. In C. Davidson (Ed.), *Minority Vote Dilution.* Washington, DC: Howard University Press.

Pettigrew, T. (1964). *A Profile of the Negro American.* Princeton, NJ: D. Van Nostrand.

Piven, F.F. & Cloward, R.A. (1977). *Poor People's Movements.* New York: Vintage.

Polsby, N. (1963). *Community Power and Political Theory.* New Haven: Yale University Press.

Preston, M.B., Henderson, L.J., Jr., & Puryear, P. (Eds.). (1982). *The New Black Politics: The Search for Political Power.* New York: Longman.

Raines, H. (1983). *My Soul Is Rested: Movement Days in the Deep South Remembered.* New York: Penguin Books. Reprint.

Ransford, H.E. & Miller, J. (1983). Race, Sex and Feminist Outlooks. *American Sociological Review, 48*, 45-59.

Reed, A.L., Jr. (1986). *The Jesse Jackson Phenomenon.* New Haven: Yale University Press.

Salaman, L.M. & Van Evera, S. (1973). Fear, Apathy, and Discrimination. *American Political Science Review, 67*, 1288-1306.

Schattschneider, E.E. (1960). *The Semisovereign People: A Realist's View of Democracy in America.* Hinsdale, IL: Dryden Press.

Sears, D.O. & McConahay, J.B. (1973). *The Politics of Violence: The New Urban Blacks and the Watts Riot.* Boston: Houghton Mifflin.

Secret, P., Johnson, J., & Welch, S. (1986). Racial Differences in Attitudes Toward School Prayer. *Social Science Quarterly, 67*, 877-886.

Seltzer, R. & Smith, R. (1985). Race and Ideology: A Research Note Measuring Liberalism and Conservatism in Black America. *Phylon, 46*, 98-105.

Sigelman, L. & Welch, S. (1984). Race, Gender, and Opinion Towards Black and Female Presidential Candidates. *Public Opinion Quarter, 48(2)* 467-475.

Simpson, G.E. & Yinger, J.M. (1985). *Racial and Cultural Minorities* (5th ed.). New York: Plenum Press.

Sites, P. & Mullins, E. (1985). The American Black Elite: 1930-1978. *Phylon, 46*, 269-280.

*Smith v. Allwright* 321 U. S. 649 (1944).

Thompson, D.C. (1974). *Sociology of the Black Experience*. Westport, CT: Greenwood Press.

U.S. Commission on Civil Rights. (1959). *Report*. Washinton, DC: U.S. Government Printing Office.

U.S. Commission on Civil Rights. (1961). *Report: Book 1, Voting*. Washington, DC: U.S. Government Printing Office.

U.S. Commission on Civil Rights (1975). *The Voting Rights Act: Ten Years After*. Washington, DC: U.S. Government Printing Office.

U.S. Commission on Civil Rights (1982). *Confronting Racial Isolation in Miami*. Washington, DC: U.S. Government Printing Office.

U.S. Kerner Commission. (1968). *The Report of the National Advisory Commission on Civil Disorders*. Washington, DC: U.S. Government Printing Office.

Verba, S. & Nie, N.H. (1972). *Participation in America*. New York: Harper and Row.

Voter Education Project. (1976). *Election Law Changes in Cities and Counties in Georgia*. Atlanta. Author.

Walton, H., Jr. (1985). *Invisible Politics*. Albany, NY: State University of New York Press.

Welch, S. & Combs, M. (1983). Interracial Differences in Opinion on Public Issues in the 1970s. *Western Journal of Black Studies, 7*, 136-141.

Welch, S. & Combs, M. (1985). Intra-Racial Differences in Attitudes of Blacks: Class Cleavages or Consensus? *Phylon, 46*, 91-97.

Welch, S. & Foster, L. (1987, October). Class and Conservatism in the Black Community. *American Politics Quarterly*.

Widick, B.J. (1972). *Detroit: City of Race and Class Violence*. Chicago: Quadrangle Books.

Williams, L. (1987). Black Political Progress in the 1980s: The Electoral Arenas. In M.B. Preston, L. Henderson, and P. Puryear (Eds.), *The New Black Politics: The Search for Political Power* (2d ed.). New York: Longman.

Wolfinger, R.E. & Rosenstone, S.J. (1980). *Who Votes?* New Haven: Yale University Press.

Zinn, H. (1964). *SNCC: The New Abolitionists*. Boston: Beacon Press.

Zipp, J.F. (1985). Perceived Representativeness and Voting. *American Political Science Review, 79*, 50-61.

# 4

# The Search for Voice: Ideology and Perspective in the Black Community

Phillip L. Clay

*Editor's note: This article was originally published in September, 1987, as Occasional Paper No. 3 by the William Monroe Trotter Institute, University of Massachusetts at Boston. A shortened version also appeared in the Fall 1987 issue of the Institute's quarterly,* The Trotter Review.

During the 1980s there was a significant shift to the right in the ideological perspectives of American political institutions and behavior. The term "moderate" has acquired a conservative meaning, and liberals have been split into neo-liberal and neo-conservative camps. Despite some inconsistencies, the direction has been clear. American society is informally declaring that it is not committed to achieving the goal of equal outcomes long-espoused by a mainly liberal national political and institutional system.

The shift to the right is creating changes in traditional black ideological perspectives, both among blacks and between black and white groups. The voices that in the past spoke for black interests, whether they came from black or white groups, no longer effectively present a clear or compelling vision for how we progress towards a just society. The lack of a coherent progressive ideology or voice is evident among blacks and whites. There is division and a lack of momentum. One result is a schism in the black community that has resulted in a loss of influence upon national policy. Blacks must articulate a new vision and formulate new and progressive approaches that respond to the current social and political realities.

The American people in general, and certainly black Americans, are not particularly ideological. There is no strong passion for ideological positions in this country as there is in some European countries and in other parts of the world. Historical evidence supports this assessment. How else, for example, could a socialist be elected (and re-elected) as mayor of a large city, Burlington, in the rural and conservative state of Vermont? How could Massachusetts at once support arch-liberal Ted Kennedy and arch-conservative Ed King? Finally, how could conservative Ronald Reagan be elected president by the majority of voters in 49 states when only a minority of those voters identify themselves as conservative and most disagree with him on major issues in economic and social policy?

This evidence is not to suggest that Americans do not have points of view. They have "informal ideologies," for example, about the role of government versus other institutions, or the extent to which government should be active in promoting social goals. But Americans are not passionate in those beliefs and are not bothered by inconsistencies between stated views and actions.

Does ideology in fact make a difference? Since our democracy has survived and prospered, and since blacks have moved steadily if not fully toward freedom under both nominally liberal and nominally conservative leadership, does it really matter that there is a certain raggedness and inconsistency in our belief systems?

I will argue in this essay that point of view is helpful in establishing political voice. Ideology is a definition of a group's perspectives, desires, and aspirations in relation to the rest of society and to other groups. Ideology reflects a position on questions regarding the relationship between state action and political, economic, and social outcomes. "Voice" is the translation of this ideology into political behaviors, positions on issues, coalitions, and so on.

The process by which competing interests are resolved is politics. The only people in a society who are really nonideological and who need no separate "voice" are those who have no interests aside from the common indivisible interest of the society. There are, in fact, few such people in America. Groups by definition have interests different from the society at large, and most Americans have membership in such groups. American history is a history of various interests being forwarded. Politics without ideology (voice) is not likely to be successful because it will not lead consistently and efficiently toward satisfying group interests in relation to those of the larger society.

In this paper, I will further argue that blacks are in a state of disarray regarding the voice with which they speak to each other and to the larger society. National black politics is currently neither efficient nor effective in articulating or advancing blacks' claims for equality in the larger society where elements still resist such claims. As we move into the 1990s, this situation threatens to become even more serious as various other groups jockey for the inclusion of their agenda in both the Republican and Democratic platforms. While debate rages about whether American society is aligning with the right–turning away from equality as a goal–blacks are not involved in the debate and are not active in making the case for their interests.

Of course, this has not always been the case. Early in this century, blacks such as Du Bois and Washington presented voices that offered alternatives for blacks. Others–from Garvey to Malcolm to King to Carmichael–also offered coherent perspectives for social and political action. They generated great debates and were central in creating institutions and movements that shaped the politics of their day.

Presently, the civil rights movement is dead; there is no national movement or forum. Even though the organizations that were once active are still in place, they are struggling to survive and to defend past gains rather than breaking new ground. Prominent black leaders are mainly politicians grounded in local constituencies. While the care and concern of blacks was once at the top of the nation's agenda and was in the stewardship of a single-minded black leadership, this leadership is now scattered and scrambling for attention in a nation increasingly unwilling to take it seriously.

Today we seem to have politics without the analysis of perspectives that should precede it. Political and policy debates are strategic and reactive rather than enlightening and proactive. More importantly, there is little formal communication within the black community about positions on the great issues of the day.

The absence of voice arising out of this lack of communication, as well as that resulting from real or imagined conflicts of interest, reflects a critical problem. The virtual absence of blacks in the intellectual debates defining or redefining the contours of America's public policy means the future is being decided with little black input. And what input there is is not being sifted through the screen of interests within the black community. Unable to rely any longer upon the power of liberalism that benefited them in the past, blacks must develop a voice of their own that correctly represents them on a national level.

## The Rightward Drift and Civil Rights

For the last 40 years this nation has enacted policies generally viewed as liberal, although it has done so sometimes reluctantly and often without passion. During this time the national government expanded its scope of services, regulations, and activities. The goal was to reduce differences between groups or regions and to protect individuals from social misfortunes, the economy, and even their own personal behavior. Ending discrimination, if not the fostering of equality, was a central goal.

While the struggle for group improvement, for advancing the general welfare, and for balancing liberty and equality is as old as the Constitution, these goals were not consistently pursued until Franklin Roosevelt put executive leadership, legislation, and regulatory muscle into the attainment of them. Between the years of the Great Depression and 1980, under presidents who were both Democrat and Republican, the federal span of activist public policy grew steadily.

Blacks benefited substantially from this expansion in government. Indeed, much of the expansion between 1960 and 1980 was directly related to the claims on government by blacks and their supporters advocating greater civil rights and economic justice. During this period, then, there was a substantial transformation in this country, the details of which I will explore a little later. Suffice it to say at this point that under this expanded federal government, the one-third of the nation's ill-housed, ill-fed, and unemployed that Roosevelt observed in 1932 was dramatically reduced. In addition, the great differences between the North and South were substantially reduced, the modernization of the South and the development of the West proceeded at a rapid pace, and America's place in the world, while interrupted by such misadventures as the war in Vietnam, expanded substantially. During this time America generated a surplus that was shared with the world at large and that contributed to making the least well off in this country better off. While the poor were still with us in the 1980s, their numbers were reduced by half compared to the prewelfare era.

Since the late 1970s, and especially in the 1980s, a variety of events combined to shift white public opinion toward the right and away from civil rights support. What have been some of the features of this trend?

Since the mid-70s our society has been aging. Whereas our's was a society that seemed to be dominated by youth in the 60s and early 70s it has become increasingly dominated by baby boom adults. In contrast to their parents and grandparents who experienced the Depression and World War II and who wanted the government to provide security against the vagaries of the market and to help their children move into a secure place in the middle class, this current young adult group has taken a different view. For them present concerns include consolidating middle-class status and increasing wealth and opportunity in a competitive context. This trend, of course, is inconsistent with the strong redistributive ethic that has more or less consistently run through American politics.

This young middle-class population has two principal traits that are important for understanding the rightward shift in our society. First, their education and training support the domination of ideas and analysis over populist or liberal sentiment—those romantic feelings based on a sense of solidarity among the oppressed or the aggrieved. The young middle class brings a mindset of technical rationality to the formation of political perspectives. Few in this group have ever experienced poverty or the fears associated with it. Theirs is and always has been a relatively comfortable life, and they have had education and experience that shows them the possibilities of increasing that comfort. Compared to earlier generations they have obtained status and comfort without much blood or sweat and they believe, subliminally at least, that everyone can obtain it. While there have been economic downturns (three recessions in the last decade-and-a-half years, for example) and some marginal losses in real income, the safety net for the middle class is a tight mesh through which few middle-class people fall.

The young middle class is suspicious of sentimentality and of the political strategies and appeals based upon it—that is, strategies and appeals like those that were dominant in their parents' era. Ex-Speaker of the House "Tip" O'Neill is a great reminder of what they don't want; George Bush and Ronald Reagan, on the other hand, look like the boss they want to please—a boss they respect even if they don't agree with him on some issues. Many young people don't remember John F. Kennedy or Martin Luther King, and they view the 1960s as an over-romanticized, chaotic, and unsettling era that they do not want to repeat. In their minds Vietnam and a poorer international competitive position crippled the image of "America the Strong" during that time. They see that the social problems aggressively attacked during the 1960s are still with us and are cynical about what is possible and who is responsible.

The second aspect of this shift to the right in the middle class is the increasing amount of competition its members face, given the large size of the baby boomer cohort. The brightest have been successful and are at a point now where they want to consolidate and compound their winnings, not reduce, share, or trivialize them. This competition further reduces sentimentality and altruism.

There are two other societal trends that help explain the shift to the right: economic restructuring and demographic change. The economic restructuring that has occurred over the past 20 years has been characterized by the decline of the heavy industrial and unionized sectors, and by the rise of small businesses and high-tech service and professional occupations. Deficits, trade imbalance, and manufacturing decline have underscored the frailties in the economy. Career advancement has become less certain for many and the chance to advance as fast as one's parents did and to obtain as much cannot be taken for granted.

There has been an increase in the professional and managerial class. While in many cases these workers are not paid more than the mature working class, they are exposed to a different set of values–values that are ideologically opposite to those of their parents, who saw workers as a class of people who were obliged to struggle against the bosses. The bosses have become heroes and are no longer villains. This change represents a major, if as yet inexplicit, shift in our society.

Economic restructuring and demographic change have combined to change dramatically the character of the liberal alliance that had been influential in recent decades. Unions are weaker and more suspect, the family farmer has virtually disappeared, and the black population is scattered over many more states and is concentrated within the larger cities, excluded from the suburbs where most of the new middle-class population grew up and now resides.

Old ethnic and immigrant groups have been assimilated and have moved away from the urban core. The shared interests in a common turf (the city) that characterized traditional political organizations and unions no longer applies. Today individuals are in a position to be (and are encouraged to be) far more independent in their judgments and their alliances. They rely less on gatekeepers, opinion leaders, and moral arbiters. Fewer institutions manage people's relationship to the larger society. It is now "in" to be an Independent rather than a Democrat or Republican.

As these developments occurred, blacks shared in some of them but not in others. For example, economic restructuring has been a major factor in the advancement of some blacks and the falling behind of others. While the black middle class has grown in an expanded industrial and service economy, the number of unemployed blacks has grown still more rapidly as that economy shifted from low-skilled jobs. The result is the evolution of an unemployable "underclass" of the permanently poor, even as a black middle class emerges. Yet many middle-class blacks remain stalwarts in the liberal alliance that is under siege from the right. At the same time, there are many blacks who are beginning to be affected by the dominance of ideas over sentiment–and, indeed, that shift explains in part the growing schism in the black community that I will discuss below.

The increasing competition in society has also affected the black community by raising tensions between black and white peers in professional and work environments over such issues as affirmative action and seniority. While whites are rushing to assert independence and eschewing "special interests" in their personal politics, blacks continue to feel obliged (but not without increasing dissent and personal tension) to continue reliance on race politics—a political stance that says blacks should reflect solidarity around the race issue to the substantial exclusion of other issues.

The trends discussed above at least partially explain the rightward political shift in this country during the last decade. How are these sentiments organized in political terms, how have they changed, and where do blacks stand with respect to them?

## The Nature of Ideology

In speaking of ideology I have several specifics in mind. I am interested in attitudes concerning the role of government and to what extent racial interests are included in government policy. I am also interested in the extent to which the complex interaction between race, class, and other features is addressed. I am interested in the extent to which the public process is open and the degree to which democratic values prevail. I will look at attitudes towards justice and the extent to which economic injustices stemming from pure market outcomes are accepted. Finally, I am interested in how the conflict between liberty and equality is resolved. The issue here is the extent to which individuals are free to pursue their own interests and to enjoy their own winnings (liberty) as compared to the extent to which public policy intervenes on behalf of the less well-off, the vulnerable, or the public generally (equality).

When we look at the major ideological perspectives on these several dimensions, we find substantial shifts among moderates and liberals to more explicitly conservative notions. Those shifts have important meaning for blacks.

For most blacks there is a clear starting point on each of these questions. Blacks have traditionally assumed that government would play a substantial role in society and that the federal government's intervention on their behalf was more dependably favorable and subject to their influence than state and local intervention. They depended on the federal government to protect their particular interests, mainly the reduction of segregation, racial inequality, and discrimination through civil rights legislation in particular and through legislation in other areas such as social welfare and administrative regulations.

Blacks have traditionally viewed the attainment of justice as a primary obligation of government and have believed that economic injustice without mitigation is unacceptable. Government responsibility in this regard, they believe, is to protect individuals from private or market outcomes that have operated to sustain or increase racial inequality. Blacks have typically experienced liberty negatively because they have seen it used to reinforce or increase their inequality—for instance in arguments about segregated neighborhoods and work places or about discrimination in public or business settings.

Blacks have traditionally aligned themselves with the politicians or parties that best reflect their activist points of view. Since the days of FDR this has generally meant the Democratic party, but in some states and elections, there have been exceptions. Even black conservatives have accepted this broad activist view, saving their conservative views for strictly economic, religious, or other nonrace related matters.

Today most politicians, parties, and ideological representatives declare that they are nonracist. They claim to promote opportunity for all, and they claim to abhor discrimination. Politicians from all points of view suggest that progress for blacks has been made, and they argue that their particular point of view will speed progress forward. Recently, a number of black conservatives have emerged and have joined in the debate. These newcomers, however, are out of step with black traditionalists (even conservative black traditionalists) who are for the most part liberal on matters related to race. These new conservatives, speaking largely from white institutions and isolated from blacks and from any political accountability, find suspicious ears in the black community. Black radicals who call for an end to the capitalist system are and have been even less regarded.

It is perhaps important to note that some of the difficulty we have noted above–and will be exploring more in the sections below–arises from the changing nature of the status of the "black problem" in America. We have moved from a problem that had at its core legal barriers to participation to a problem that has economic inequality at its core. Fighting racial barriers that were specifically illegal was easy compared to challenging the distribution of socioeconomic outcomes that are not constitutionally guaranteed. A major reason for the evolving nonrole of blacks in American politics is the failure of black politics and politics in general to factor in the different issues involved.

## Varieties of Belief

In the sections below I will discuss varieties of liberal, conservative, and radical points of view and the issues raised in each of them on the matter of race. In undertaking this, however, there are some caveats. The first is that any attempt at cataloging these perspectives runs the risk of oversimplifying. Simplifications are, of course, unavoidable in any kind of discourse, and, therefore, we ought not back away; simplification is also a useful foil for complexity.

Secondly, as I noted in the beginning, Americans are not temperamentally ideological. There are within most Americans some points of view that are inconsistent with a dominant perspective. It is also true that not everyone acts on their beliefs. We are often constrained by institutional, contextual, or personal affection. Whites may be hostile to aspirations of blacks as a group but not to the aspirations of individual blacks or of blacks they know or come to know well. Blacks who grew up in the South are well aware of these contradictions.

## Liberals

The liberal tradition goes back to the age of reform that had its origins in the nineteenth century, flourished in the progressive era, and triumphed with the election of President Franklin Roosevelt in 1932. The liberal ideology is founded on the belief that humans are perfectible and that a more perfect and humane society can be achieved. Liberals (generally referring to whites) believe they understand society and understand how to make society more perfect. Blacks have been the beneficiaries of liberal reform attention.

This notion of the good society is best obtained, according to the liberal point of view, through a strong central government and through regulation of both the economy and areas of personal behavior that are deemed important for the general good of society, especially for the good of those less well-off. Liberals accept capitalism and the market, but they do not accept the system's failure to protect or uplift the poor. They acknowledge that the market will not eliminate poverty, but they feel that redistribution can substantially reduce the suffering in society and make it possible for most people to gain access to the expanding economic pie that the free market promises. They favor government policies that are compensatory or partly redistributive as an antidote to economic injustice. Perfect equality has never been a liberal goal.

Liberals have advocated intervention by both public and private spheres. The liberal view is that government should act positively to achieve outcomes rather than to simply set a tone. On busing, for example, liberals believe that the result to be achieved (integrated education) justifies government action even though that action violates the liberty that same government also espouses. Liberals have a similar view with respect to group versus individual treatment. Given their belief in the possibility of a more perfect society, they are inclined to promote public policy that benefits groups rather than individuals.

Given this general outlook, the liberal attitude towards blacks is not hard to detect. It is reflected in the use of the central government and other institutions to benefit blacks as a group and to produce results rather than simply opportunities for results. The tactical approach of liberals has been to create and support various interest groups and organizations that are a part of their coalition. Such groups exist for blacks as they do for labor, public education, health, progressive farming, and other interests. Liberals have never been a homogeneous group, but rather a collection of special interest groups that have in common the notion of actively creating a better society. Inconsistencies between the interests of these special groups have generally been sublimated, and their overarching goal of a just society emphasized.

In their treatment of blacks liberals tend to be democratic, but they reserve for themselves the status of senior partners in liberal institutions and movements. In some cases paternalism characterizes the liberal's relationship with blacks. The pattern is present in personal relationships and most especially in institutional ones. While liberalism was the dominant influence between 1930 and 1980, many would contend that liberals have never really been in full command or confident about their power. Even during the depths of the Depression, liberals were on the defensive. This was in large part because their view of social engineering is inconsistent with the dominant American ethos that emphasizes individual traditions and values. As a result, liberals have often been forced to camouflage their social engineering motives and adopt some of the platitudes of conservatives.

In recent years, as the conservative assault has broadened and increased, liberals have been put even more on the defensive. Their confidence has sagged under the weight of several electoral losses dating back to 1968. No liberal has been elected president since Johnson and some of the country's most dependable and eloquent liberal politicians have been defeated. Perhaps not surprisingly, many surviving liberals are thus taking steps toward the center of the political spectrum.

Black voices in liberal circles have been mainly political as opposed to intellectual. As liberals have had to face challenges to their point of view and policies, blacks have lent much political and moral support, but little in the way of revision or revitalization. During the 1980s, when many books, studies, and papers were written as part of the public policy debate, there were very few black entries. It is as though blacks are the noncommissioned officers in the liberal core. This second-class citizenship, or intellectual isolation, remains a source of real tension, especially to young blacks, even though the "black power" rhetoric that first gave voice to that tension has subsided.

Equality was well served during the years of liberal dominance. Practically no one would dispute that progress has been made in bringing blacks into the mainstream. But success has been far from complete. Many of the problems that blacks have always complained about are still obstacles. In recent years the tensions and conflicts among various liberal interest groups have dominated liberal political dialogue and public discourse. These have included disagreements on affirmative action, seniority, community control, and Democratic party rules and have engendered a good deal of disenchantment among those who still profess to be liberals. This tension has also led to the emergence of both neo-liberals and neo-conservatives. The disenchantment with the shifting agenda and the disaffection (or perceived disaffection) of once-faithful friends is the source of much anguish in the black and liberal communities.

While some liberals have sought to reassess their policy perspective in light of new realities and have as a result come up with new proposals that are still consistent with the liberal ideology (Governor Cuomo may be considered an example in this regard), many others have taken detours from the traditional liberal path. Hence we have the emergence of the neo-liberals and the neo-conservatives.

## Neo-Liberals

Neo-liberals are liberals who have taken a look at the traditional liberal approaches, alliances, and perspectives on public policy issues that they regarded as automatic and obligatory and decided that they should be subject to critical review. Charles Peters, author of *Neo-Liberal Manifesto* (1983) writes:

> ...if neoconservatives are liberals who took a critical look at liberalism and decided to become conservatives, we are liberals who took the same look and decided to retain our goals but to abandon some of our prejudices. We still believe in liberty and justice and a fair chance for all, in the mercy for the afflicted and help for the down and out. But we no longer favor unions and big government or are opposed to military and big business. Indeed for our solutions to work we have come to distrust all automatic responses–liberal and conservative. (p. 12)

The neo-liberals have some points of view that put them at odds with the liberal mainstream and with blacks. For example, they do not favor industrial policy that seeks to revive or protect the old industries (in which lots of blacks work and to which access has been recent), but rather seek to promote growth-oriented entrepreneurship and small business, not simply to shuffle assets as in speculation, mergers, and the like. They are prodefense but not proforeign intervention and they accept social program cuts as necessary and acceptable in the current effort to control deficits. They favor the use of economic sanctions but not military intervention. They oppose protectionist policies. They are against big labor and big government but they are not opposed to unions or government intervention.

They believe that government should be strong but not big, and that government should figure out what it should do and do those things efficiently and well. They believe that government should avoid those things it cannot do effectively even if attention to them is clearly merited. They are more excited by government that serves as public entrepreneur and regulator of incentives for development than as big-muscled social engineer.

Neo-liberals specifically reject "special interests" and favor government as an agent of the public interest. They regard as "special interests" those groups that make up the liberal alliance–unions, gay rights activists, the education lobby, trade protectionists, etc. Blacks resent the "special interest" prejudice as it is attached to civil rights and antipoverty activists, arguing that seeking justice is hardly the same thing as seeking a tax loophole, exclusive subsidies, trade protection, or other such economic benefits at the public's expense.

While neo-liberals assert that they have an interest in enforcing civil rights laws, they do not believe that they have an obligation to accept demands for equal outcomes. They do not regard equal outcomes as fundamentally or reasonably achievable, and they are committed only to making opportunity equally available to the extent that it is "possible" and to do so by "expanding the pie."

They do not believe that all criminals can be rehabilitated or that all kids should go to Harvard. And they claim that they can figure out how to make choices. They believe, with respect to criminals for example, that since you can't rehabilitate them, you should at least lock them up. While they favor educational opportunities, they are not inclined to undo the elitist bias reflected in many educational systems and policies.

Neo-liberals are empathetic to social issues raised by conservatives where liberals often are not. For example, while they oppose mandatory prayer in schools, they might not object to a nonsectarian "moment of silence." They favor desegregation but do not feel obliged to support busing. In short they want to update liberalism, making it appeal to the young middle-class constituency. They are not sentimental about, nor defensive about, having abandoned the old liberal stand on the side of the downtrodden.

While some of these departures from traditional views are matters of degree and emphasis, some shake what might be called liberal articles of faith. Neo-liberals fought liberals on aid to Chrysler. Neo-liberals are more positive on tuition tax credits. They are not as protectionist as liberal union advocates. Gary Hart, their presidential standard-bearer in 1984, got few endorsements from traditional liberal or black groups who considered his technical, rational approaches cold. Bradley, Gephardt, Babbitt, and Nunn faced similar skepticism.

Neo-liberals do not have a party. Indeed they do not have a movement. They are a loose collection of journalists, academics, writers, and politicians. Unlike their traditional liberal colleagues, they place a great deal of emphasis on rational analysis in addressing public policy questions. They like "new ideas," by which they mean policies that define a role for government that is effective, unsentimental, and based on leveraging constructive individual and collective motives. They believe the government should support entrepreneurship, competition, and partnership as effective tools to help those in need.

There's a hard edge—some might say arrogance—to the neo-liberal position. They seem uncomfortable dealing with racial issues and in working with or being politically collegial with those who do not share their middle-class background. Indeed blacks are suspicious of neo-liberals because neo-liberals object to "special interests" and to traditional litmus tests blacks might apply. It is not surprising, therefore, that between the two leading white Democratic contenders in 1984, blacks overwhelmingly preferred Walter Mondale, the traditional liberal, to Gary Hart, the neo-liberal.

For blacks, the issue is not simply the neo-liberal view on specific policy issues. In fact, many of the black middle class may find that they agree with neo-liberals on many particulars. The concerns many blacks share about this brand of political ideology focus on other matters:

- Neo-liberals are often unwilling to give a preamble of commitment to equality or equal outcomes as a goal for government policy;

- Neo-liberals prefer attention to the middle class and not the underclass;

- Neo-liberals prefer analysis to sentiment, which effectively marginalizes black political expression that is not analytically presented;

- Neo-liberals express abhorrence for "special interests," among which are blacks and other liberal support groups; and

- Neo-liberals support entrepreneurship and the private sector and are skeptical of what expanding government can do to improve society.

What some middle-class blacks who might share these positions fear is that coalition with the neo-liberals will further divide blacks along class lines and consign poor blacks to an "underclass" with little power and no effective or competent political allies–black or white. Beyond this there is the question of how and whether neo-liberalism can move from marginalism to the partnership that young blacks insist on as a condition for support. Neo-liberals presently show but limited disposition in this regard.

Neo-liberals are very active in the effort to reorganize the Democratic party, and they may well prevail in shaping the party to their image. Indeed, they believe that the Democratic party can only succeed if it adopts their point of view and recaptures from Republicans the young white moderates who they believe make up the largest sector in the voting population. Neo-liberals are an ascendant force in the mainstream of American politics. They view dealing with black aspirations and sentimentality as undesirable and unnecessary. While neo-liberals do not currently dominate the mainstream of the Democratic party's organization, that is surely changing in their favor. The issues that divide them from traditional liberals will form the debate about the direction of the party for decades to come.

Blacks have yet to develop a response to the neo-liberal challenge or to figure out how to deal with the growing influence of these ideological insurgents. The major battleground to date has been the Democratic party rules. The class difference between blacks and neo-liberal activists is significant, as are their styles. Blacks have not figured out how to get the neo-liberals' attention–what to say to them about programs and about the goals viewed as sacred by blacks and liberals. Recent Democratic victories and Republican weakness have given new momentum to the party. How blacks get beyond party rules and into substantive platform issues will be an important political drama.

## Conservatives

What do conservatives believe? The primary tenet that conservatives bring to the table is a belief in the free market as the primary arbiter of interests, ideas, and values in American society. For them the market is also the principal allocator among competing groups. They believe that the market, if left alone, will provide the greatest benefits to the most people. Conservatives favor self-reliance and individual effort rather than group strategies to achieve the benefits of the marketplace.

Where social policy is necessary, they favor attention to individuals and not to groups. In fact, they deplore the idea of group interests, whereas the treatment of group interest has always been central to blacks. Conservatives also believe that a strong central government is inimical to the interests of the majority. They favor action at the lowest level of government with fewer functions provided at the central or national level. They believe in education, for example, but not that there be a national standard or that government be obliged to help poor people use education to reduce inequality. They believe that the "bells and whistles" in society are for the private sector and local foundations to address, or for individuals to purchase.

They believe in liberty–the idea that people are free to enjoy the benefits of their accumulated wealth and power as well as free from government constraint in social affairs. Conservatives believe that these liberties should not be comprised so as to be redistributed to those who have less. They believe in "traditional family values" and that intervention in individual behavior is only justified when that behavior is by its nature evil. Thus, some conservatives favor government action to prevent abortions because they believe abortion is fundamentally wrong. On the other hand, they do not believe, for example, that segregation is an evil for which busing (a constraint on liberty) ought to be the solution. They believe freedom of choice is adequate to meet the constitutional requirement of equal protection of the law as well as their notion of social responsibility.

In race relations, conservatives believe that government should support equal opportunity but not require or even encourage equal results. They believe the market will determine what the results ought to be and that market-generated results ought to be accepted as the most efficient and most fair. Anyone who feels unsatisfied by the market result ought, therefore, by individual action seek to change the results for themselves. Conservatives generally are opposed to policies that are race-conscious, including strong affirmative action plans.

Conservatives argue that, historically, social programs sponsored by liberals substantially failed and interfered with the incentives blacks would otherwise have had to take advantage of market opportunities and incentives. In that vein, they conclude that the programs were harmful or wrong, or both. They feel that the economic tide will, in fact, lift all boats and that blacks' entrance into the mainstream is their only opportunity for equality.

Conservatives would argue that discrimination is not a serious problem since in the free marketplace discrimination is irrational. Personal preferences, they argue, are acceptable. While conservatism is not by definition racist, it does provide an umbrella under which racial discrimination, dressed in institutional rules and personal preference, can hide.

It appears that a growing number of blacks are articulating conservative points of view. This is new as a journalistic phenomenon but is not new in fact. There has always been a conservative streak among blacks. What sets the traditional black conservatives apart from newer ones, such as Thomas Sowell, Glenn Loury, and Walter Williams, is the latter group's opposition to certain civil rights laws and their belief that social and economic policy ought not explicitly be designed to reduce racial equality or give special attention to race. They assume what is good for the economy is good for blacks. Indeed black conservatives have become some of the most impassioned critics of race-conscious public policy, including affirmative action. White conservatives and young black conservatives have joined to argue that advocacy on a racial basis and on the basis of group membership is fundamentally wrong.

Of course there are varieties of conservative belief. At the one extreme, libertarians argue that to pursue the goals described above, government ought to do little if anything beyond national defense and public health and safety. More moderate conservatives, on the other hand, accept that government has some responsibility in social areas, such as when the market falls to such an extent that there is a threat to social stability. All conservatives believe that stability is a requirement for justice, not that justice is a requirement for stability, as liberals argue.

## Neo-Conservatives

Neo-conservatives are former liberals who looked at the liberal political traditions and chose to become conservative rather than becoming neo-liberal. They reject the core of liberal beliefs. They react to many of the same issues and concerns that prompted neo-liberals to make their switch. Examples of neo-conservatives include: Irving Kristol (editor of *Public Interest*), Nathan Glazer (*Affirmative Discrimination*, 1975), and Edward Banfield (*The Unheavenly City*, 1974). Neo-conservatives are for the most part intellectuals. They are primarily located in research institutions and universities and most are older men. Some are former radicals as well as former liberals.

They share neo-liberal reactions to the automatic sentiments of liberals and the conservative's respect for the power and fairness of the market as social arbiter and economic allocator. They also believe strongly in traditional social values. They interpret the shortcomings of social programs and the rise of the black middle class as proof that the traditional liberal approach to social engineering is fundamentally wrong, ineffective (for those still in need), and unnecessary (for blacks who are now middle class).

Unlike neo-liberals, neo-conservatives do not have an activist view or an alternative to the free market route to the more perfect society or the more just society. Neo-conservatives view society as fundamentally just. From their point of view, further perfection is not likely to result from social engineering. Wilson and Heinstein's *Crime and Human Nature* (1986), for example, ascribes to the nature of criminals the behavior liberals have blamed on society for our imperfect institutions. This neo-conservative critique of criminal justice concludes that much social and criminal justice policy ought to be scrapped. Similar critiques have been made in the welfare and education areas.

Neo-conservatives react angrily, like a scorned parent, to what they consider to be the excesses of the 60s and 70s–particularly to the race-related concessions and preferences of that period. They have a high regard for culture, intelligence, self-reliance, civility, and good manners as evidence of mature behavior and responsible political stewardship. Unlike neo-liberals they feel no obligation to search for a means to accommodate the democratic process to those who have no such background or standards. For neo-conservatives the vote and related political institutions are sufficient forms of access.

Unlike neo-liberals, who are essentially positivists and rational analysts, neo-conservatives are in simple terms fed up with social engineering. They are uncomfortable with civil rights and racial advocacy and, indeed, many of them have made declarations that have in effect trivialized race. For example, Patrick Moynihan more than a decade ago suggested that the issue of race would benefit from a period of "benign neglect." Nathan Glazer has described many of the traditional social programs advocated by liberals and blacks to be clear examples of "affirmative discrimination" in addition to being misguided and counterproductive.

As neo-conservatives are uncomfortable with current civil rights issues, so blacks are especially uncomfortable with neo-conservatives. Indeed they find neo-conservatives far more unapproachable and insensitive on matters of race than the traditional conservatives, who often can be convinced to be race interventionists for a variety of reasons (related to "social stability" or "corporate responsibility").

Neo-conservatives are disenchanted and unsympathetic with racial and social activism. There is little hope that they will seek partnership with the black masses. They are not key actors in many institutions and, with few exceptions, they are "national critics"–political actors without any base at the state or local level.

While neo-conservatives are not politically active as a group, their influences should not be underestimated. They write books and appear on television. They are highly literate and as such are effective in the media. Especially important is the fact that they create "ideas in good currency" and provide analysis that has the effect of giving voice to ideas that the political conservatives and neo-liberal actors share. The influence of Charles Murray's *Losing Ground* (1984) is illustrative in this regard. They are also influential in the institutions that play an important role in society, especially the university.

The fact that blacks are not involved in the discussions conducted by neo-conservatives and are not present when the arguments are made in scholarly and institutional settings means that the social policy revisions in government are often developed without black input at critical stages. Congress, which used to be a forum for the debate of domestic social policy, was reduced in the 1980s to a forum for Reagan's fiscal and economic approach to undermining liberal social policy.

### Radicals

My observations about radicals will not be extensive or comprehensive. This is not to suggest that they are not deserving of some discussion or that their contrasting beliefs are not important. It is just that they are not now nor have they ever been in the political mainstream. Unlike European countries where the ideological fringe often has influence and presence, such is not the case here.

The various radical critiques are important, however. For example, among all the ideologies, radicals have cogent, if not always compelling, explanatory models that speak to the old and continuing sources of inequalities between the races. Radicals generally argue against concentrated private power and wealth, lack of public control, and repressive restrictions on self-determination and self-definition. While they are often naive about what can be done in various areas of public policy, their diagnostic insights are sharp.

They argue that New Deal liberalism, more recent liberal policies, and the market have all failed to bring about the economic redistribution that is their definition of social justice. They believe that the growth of the middle class has made revolutionary and radical change less likely because the constituency for redistribution has eroded. They contend that mainstream efforts to bring about change, such as bargaining, marginal shifts-in-share of resources, and pressure group politics will fail in the future as they have in the past. They are perhaps most critical of liberals because they argue that liberals are fundamentally cowards, recognizing and agreeing with the sociopolitical dynamics that radicals assert but unwilling to accept the implications of this knowledge.

However well worked out, the radical perspective has been marginal in the practice of public management. For that reason radicals generally have not had a central place in American politics and have not attracted substantial black interest. In the current ideological turmoil that seems to be even more the case. The declining influence of radicals (black or white) in the black community is not surprising. Black intellectuals have long been disillusioned with radicals who, they believe, have used blacks as "victims on display," having more interest in the class than the racial aspects of inequality. Since class inequality is still the principal interest of radicals, there is likely to remain a significant distance between blacks and radicals.

The "black power movement" of the late 1960s was a case where blacks sought to make their own radical critique of American *and* black society. It is not a coincidence that a major part of this effort was that it sought to present a black radical critique separate from the white radical perspective. The movement was successful in this regard and had the impact of changing a generation of young blacks by opening up for critical examination many of the assumptions, symbols, and ideas about American society and themselves that blacks had simply adopted uncritically from the liberal tradition. Because it largely addressed issues only touched by the civil rights movement, the black power movement was important not so much for its political impact as much as for its creation of a disposition among blacks to acknowledge the importance of the questions we propose in this essay.

The black power movement succeeded in other ways as well. For instance, out of it came a new generation of political and community leaders. These leaders were different from the traditional race politicians. They were more confident and less compromising. However, insecurities and confusion remained to a troublesome degree, and the black power movement has come to a premature end. The movement was radical mainly for its insistence that blacks could demand self-determination. It was not able, however, to deal with all the applications or implications of a black perspective and thus did not leave behind a significant political institution that could perform the functions of a political party, interest group, or social movement or produce an effective and enduring progressive voice for leadership at the national level. It failed to produce any model for relating to existing political parties, identifying and articulating issues, supporting candidates and choosing among them, or managing accountability. It provided no way to interpret and adjust to the changing political and social realities. When critics comment about lack of institutional political sophistication among blacks, they are substantially correct.

It is true that a new generation of black politicians has succeeded. Most of them, however, are bogged down in their own personal and political balancing act—between the race politics that elected them and the political mainstreams through which they must swim if they are to survive. Jesse Jackson is one exception, but only in the sense that as a national candidate he is reaching for the rainbow and not articulating a voice and developing an institution for black Americans.

What I have tried to show in the preceding sections is the ideological turmoil in the politics of both the national community and the black community. This turmoil is healthy. What is unhealthy is the failure of the black community to locate a progressive voice with which to develop an agenda and carry on a dialogue. While national leaders are coming up with new perspectives about the black community and the problems it faces, the black community is not coming up with alternative or confirming perspectives and is not defending its largely liberal interests against the conservative onslaught and liberal desertion. Such disarray is not likely to be lost on presidential candidates who, amidst such disarray, can neglect black interests without repercussions by being polite and attentive to symbols and by organizing sympathetic blacks. While such a candidate may win the black vote, the black presence will be minor even if black votes play a major role. The results of such elections are certainly not lost on the poor who figure the election is not about them anyway.

## The Schism in the Black Community

The failure of voice in the black community is not an academic matter. There is every evidence that the black community is at one of those critical points in history where we are not clear about what our problems are or how to address them. We are under siege even with respect to past "victories." There are widely divergent suggestions from others about what we should do, and there are discordant demands within the community. Do blacks believe that affirmative action really is a good idea or does it place a stigma on blacks? Is busing an effective way to equalize educational opportunity or would some approach not focusing on integration be better? Should we get "tough" with crime or wait until "causes" are addressed? Does welfare promote "dependency?" What should be done about teen-age pregnancy? About gentrification?

Our leadership seems incapable of mounting either an effective defense or a credible offense. While the old divisions in the black community continue, new divisions are emerging, especially between the interests and perspectives of the expanding black middle class and the even more rapidly expanding "underclass."

## History of the Schism

The history of the schism in the black community is tied to changing economic conditions in the country. At the turn of the century, more than 90% of the black population lived in the South. They provided the muscle for the largely unmechanized agrarian system. Starting with the Depression, the old agrarian society went into a steep decline. Mechanization forced many blacks off farms; those who stayed had an increasingly marginal existence.

Starting with the mobilization for World War II, large numbers of blacks headed North. By the end of this exodus (in the mid-1960s), half of the black population lived outside the South, concentrated in two dozen large industrial cities in the North. The move mainly involved low-income blacks with limited education and training. At that time a huge gap existed between blacks and whites in terms of education. During the last two decades that gap has narrowed considerably, and, among younger black families, so has the gap in income. Those who made the most progress in this regard became the new black middle class—either by getting a "good job" in a unionized industry or through education.

The majority of blacks, however, found cities less effective as engines of opportunity than did those immigrants who had moved to American cities in large numbers throughout the century. By the 1960s the shifting economic structure of the country resulted in a declining number of manufacturing jobs that could provide middle-class status to blacks, as it had provided for generations of white working-class families. Increasingly, the city as a lever for upward mobility seemed ineffective for all but the well-educated who could take advantage of the growing number of white-collar-job opportunities. By the 1980s, when large numbers of young blacks came of age and lower-paid service jobs dominated, the trend that had been set in motion in the 60s became even more apparent.

Blacks also found at this time that in cities the opportunities in the public sector were on the decline. The public sector had provided opportunities for some immigrant groups to gain a foothold in the city and improve their economic status by their demographic and subsequently electoral domination. This was not true for blacks, even though black political control did eventually come to several large cities. In terms of public sector jobs, though, blacks were essentially competing for a share of a shrinking pie.

Finally, because race is a special and indelible mark of oppression, blacks were not able to melt into the urban stew. Mounting racial tension, highlighted by the "unrest" of the 1960s, meant that every effort blacks made to improve their position set them up for conflict with whites who were left behind or who had come to feel entitled to their exclusive but shrinking prerogatives. Jobs that could help the black poor advance became increasingly unavailable during the 70s and 80s, and high rates of unemployment, especially for young black workers, seemed to remain at high levels whatever the state of the economy as a whole.

By 1960 the contours of status differences–blacks versus whites–were already clear. While some cities such as Atlanta, Washington, New York, and Chicago were able to develop a large black middle class that could in fact generate its own growth, this was by far the exception. And in no city was the black population like the white population–mainly middle class. Blacks were more than twice as likely to be poor, and their unemployment rate was at least twice the unemployment rate of whites, regardless of education. By 1980 these contours had hardened, and scholars began to talk about the black poor not as a fractional phenomenon but as a class–an "underclass." The country had a small but growing group of middle-class blacks who were doing well, and a larger and also growing group of poor blacks who were struggling to make do, if that.

What does it mean when there are significant changes in the two ends of the distribution of families within the black community? I come to the conclusion that this schism heightens the divergence of interests that the groups have. This divergence, in addition to producing blurred policy visions, complicates the search for an articulate and effective progressive voice.

### The Underclass

The "underclass" comprises the approximately one-third of black families in this country who earn less than $10,000 a year. Of these the 18% of black families who earn less than $5,000 are of special concern. Half of this group is not in the job market and, therefore, does not benefit from economic growth. They are–and this is an important part of the definition of "underclass"–outside of the mainstream. Some do succeed and work their way out of poverty, but this is increasingly the exception.

People in this class are not simple carbon copies of their parents, who are typically poor. Each generation is structurally poor for different reasons. Today the average young adult poor person has education and skills that in an earlier generation would have been sufficient for steady employment and decent pay. But while these individuals have gained a little more education than their parents, their greater education has come to count for less. Since the majority of all poor individuals are children, the future of these coming generations turns on the extent to which these youngsters get leverage in terms of educational preparation. They, arguably, are not getting it in the big city school systems. Racism is partly to blame, but there are economic and perhaps cultural explanations as well.

Our nation's efforts to help the underclass have been substantially unsuccessful in lifting them out of poverty: we have not conquered racism; the economic system reinforces class divisions; and we have been unwilling to devise a cultural technology that all groups, including blacks, could use when facing major obstacles.

This is not to suggest that programs have been unsuccessful generally, as conservative and neo-liberal critics increasingly charge. Many of these families would be far worse off were the safety net not available; and many presently in the middle class, over the period of a generation, did move successfully from the working class to the middle class, or in some cases from the lower class to the middle class, as a result of various social programs. In our current policy-bashing frame of mind, we should not forget that no one ever walks out of the ghetto. One is either lifted out or climbs out.

Perhaps what is important to recognize is that as the number of poor blacks continues to expand, permanence rather than instability increasingly characterizes this status. They are increasingly not being given, and to some extent are not taking advantage of, opportunities for upward mobility.

The underclass presents problems in other ways that are of growing concern. Several major cities have had comebacks in terms of job production and economic development. There has been a veritable economic renaissance in major cities such as Boston, New York, and San Francisco. Rust Belt states such as Ohio and Michigan are also showing signs of progress. While manufacturing jobs continue to decline, there has been an increase in a variety of other sectors. Some analysts now contemplate labor shortages in some cities. Their studies also show, however, that so far little mobility out of poverty has resulted from this economic resurgence. Analyses of job opportunities suggest that blacks are being locked out of the recovery growth at increasing rates; jobs are being "taken" by process changes and automation and by suburbanites and, in some locations, immigrants. What is left for poor blacks are jobs that are even more "dead-end" than the manufacturing jobs that have been lost in recent years–jobs that pay less and offer less hope for mobility.

All of this reinforces the notion of permanence of the black underclass. It also underscores the point that the present crisis of the underclass is not entirely historical but, in important ways, contemporary.

## The Black Middle Class

Approximately 18% of black households are middle class. Using the cutoff of $25,000 per year in 1979, this figure is up from 13% in 1970 and compares with a shift from 31% to 37% for whites in the same time period. The black middle-class population that we are talking about is a working middle class. Only 1% of black families (versus 6% for whites) earn as much as $50,000.

This black middle-class status is disproportionately achieved by having a working spouse and is concentrated in heads-of-household under the age of forty. Much of this middle class is new, therefore, and arrived through salaried employment in the professions rather than self-employment or business enterprise.

There are several points about this group that inform our current debate, and I will discuss them in turn. The first is that historically the black middle class has not been able to be secure in its middle-class status. Unlike middle-class whites, whose children are almost all certain to be middle class when they grow up, blacks experience no such certainty. Many older blacks experienced an unstable career trajectory that sometimes included downward mobility or stunted growth. As a result there is concern among the black middle class about how they can secure their own status as well as about how to pass it on to their own children.

This new black middle class has moved to suburbs in the last several years at a rate greater than whites. This, combined with regional mobility, means that a growing physical isolation is developing: the middle class is the suburbs (and middle-class city neighborhoods) and the underclass is the ghetto. The natural alliance cemented by propinquity and kinship is now broken by regional mobility and segregated housing. This segregation makes "us" and "them" categories easier and more concrete.

There is also within the black middle class a substantial amount of stress. The evidence for this is anecdotal but substantial. The popular black press, once consumed with interpreting and advocating civil rights and "black power," now focuses on black middle-class family, professional, and business issues–not just the petty bourgeoisie or "yuppie" issues, but investment, relationships, leadership, and entrepreneurship. The growth in the status of many young blacks has been so fast that many have serious struggles around how to juggle many parts of their life, how to interpret their success, how to feel and act towards the less fortunate of their brethren left behind, and how to deal with complex relationships they have with their white peers and bosses. This stress should not be interpreted as either a sign that they are not capable of coping or that middle-class whites don't have the same concerns; it is only to suggest that the newness of their status requires some attention and makes understandable some of the concerns we hear about the growing overlap of issues between this group and their white peers. When there is overlap, the pull of the two worlds on the individual black is truly powerful.

Another theme in the black press is the anguish over the underclass: how to solve the still-serious problems, how to use black institutions that reflect the class issues, how to relate politically and socially to the underclass, and how to protect the underclass from the moral cutbacks they sense among whites. Among middle-class blacks there is sympathy, anger, and embarrassment in good measure, directed both at whites and at their underclass brothers and sisters.

Another point to be made about the black middle class is that it is disproportionately concentrated in the industrial sector and the public sectors where the rate of future job growth is not expected to be substantial. There are relatively few blacks who are employed in engineering or technical fields or who are in the executive levels of growth-oriented service or corporate organizations. The issues of security and upward mobility among middle-class blacks depend critically on their moving quickly to consolidate their personal and class position and to make appropriate lateral and/or vertical exits to more growth-oriented sectors.

Despite their middle-class status, this group is more than twice as likely to experience unemployment as their white peers. While their unemployment rate is not high, typically 5% or so, the fact that it is twice as high as their white counterparts and that upward mobility is a problem reinforces the point that discrimination and separate treatment are important even at this level.

What is the significance of this class division between blacks of different socioeconomic status as compared to difference in perspective and experience between broader groups of "haves" and "have nots"? The evidence seems to suggest there is a growing division of interests within a group, such as blacks, that traditionally had interests that were indivisible and monolithic. For blacks the tradition of solidarity grounded in social victimization was formerly not complicated by class. The objective evidence of class was insignificant compared to the brutal and common victimization as members of a racial group. Both classes of blacks now have major concerns that require a different kind of attention. The black community's language, institutions, and forums do not reflect this fact or facilitate a solution. How, then, is this phenomenon of class schism related to the present political and ideological issues?

There are several areas where the two worlds described above collide with the larger world of policy politics. The language of that discussion (or the lack of one) and the balancing of interests and advocacy in the black community are themes of this essay. There are issues of public policy where the battle is not only strategic, but also ideological–especially regarding help for the underclass. These issues include: interdependence of interests, the nature of the "safety net," government intervention to promote a class standard (read: middle-class standard), the role of local institutions versus government, spokesmanship for blacks in political and institutional arenas.

First, it is important to acknowledge that the two classes have interdependent interests in more ways than we generally acknowledge. For instance, the middle class uses the starkly graphic suffering of the poor to gain benefits from whites that the poor are not in a position to use. It is not a put-down to suggest that affirmative action has been most beneficial to middle-class (and working-class) blacks who were prepared to enter the new doors that were opened by it. Except by some quite limited "trickle down" effect, these programs have not helped the mobility of the poor. The varying electoral clout of the poor masses is often placed in service of this strategy.

The poor depend on the middle class to both work the system for them and to provide institutional leadership in the communities. A significant proportion of the black middle class works in settings where they can be helpful to the poor, provided the resources are in place. These professional blacks are rarely in situations where they are able to fully define the agenda or allocate resources. They mainly run programs or provide services whose design originates elsewhere. In some settings where black control seems substantial (for example, urban school systems or public housing authorities), blacks in positions of relative authority are accountable to bureaucratic or official systems that often make their administration indistinguishable from that of white bureaucrats.

These interdependencies are not fully in effect. The middle class says that the poor don't vote, and the poor say that the middle class is out for itself and turns its back on them. There is clearly evidence that both points are true in part and each side offers excuses: the poor ask "Why vote?" and the middle class say the poor won't help themselves and often behave counterproductively.

The second issue is the nature of the "safety net." It goes without saying that the underclass is in need of government benefits, both for immediate survival and to obtain mobility out of the ghetto. Children, the major beneficiaries (along with the elderly) of social programs, need them merely to survive. Yet we are in a period where there are serious budget problems and a legislative mandate (Gramm-Rudman-Hollings) to reduce government spending. Programs have been cut and choices will have to continue to be made among existing programs. Certainly, there is little momentum to launch major new programs.

Both the media and political discussion suggest that there is growing doubt among the middle class about the ability of the existing welfare system to do more than maintain the poor in a dependent relationship at the level of survival. There is also a growing view that welfare ought to contain incentives that benefit those who behave in ways conforming to middle-class expectations and deprive those who do not. These are elements of a moral judgment, of a view that welfare ought to be a means to regulate the poor.

This movement is clearly in the opposite direction from that of the past 20 years of social policy, which tried with some success to make public assistance a benefit granted without moral judgment and without penalty for counterproductive behavior. Do we go back to the idea of helping out the good and grateful, or do we continue with the idea of not tying assistance to certain behavioral requirements? Workfare is a first approximation of this new direction. In recent years it has gained wide support across the political spectrum. Ten years ago, practically no one left of center favored it. This and other policies (proposals for restrictions on unwed mothers, presumptive sentencing, etc.) are now broadly favored even by middle-class blacks and will continue to be a source of division within the black community and between blacks and others.

The third point takes the issue of standards of behavior a step further by asking what standards apply in setting local and institutional policies within communities. Up to now even middle-class blacks have resisted the notion that the black community should be required to adopt middle-class standards (read: white middle-class standards). While it is never made clear what standards are being talked about, the notion is that there are cultural differences among racial and ethnic groups and that blacks need not make wholesale changes simply to conform. Variety is both acceptable and a statement of group self-determination.

There is now an emerging view, though not a new one, that some of the lower-class black lifestyles are pathological and ought to change. If the black middle class, whose standards are similar to those of their white peers, begins to share this view, we again have the basis for a conflict in point of view–with a conflict about social policies close behind. Policies in the area of families, education, and criminal justice, as well as the tone and character of activities within black organizations and agencies, will reflect this tension. The black middle class that runs these programs and agencies will be on the front line as managers of a process by which external standards are forced on the poor. To this point, the black middle class has resisted this role, but there is rethinking and there may well be reform that changes this policy. Blacks have not figured out a position on this, and it will certainly come up in Democratic platform debates.

Embedded in these issues is the potential for division within the ranks of the black middle class with those in the service professions who adhere to race politics and a liberal social policy on one side and younger, more conservative blacks with their neo-liberal (or "pragmatic liberal") colleagues on the other side.

Another policy issue is who will take the lead in shaping social programs and public policies–the federal government, local government, or nongovernment institutions, including those in the black community? The role of the federal government will be a major issue in the next election. It is unlikely that the federal government will have no role to play in these matters since they are the only branch capable of making major income and resource transfers. It seems likely that more and more state and local discretion will be exercised, so that many important program design and implementation issues will be settled at the local level.

The black middle class and their liberal friends are in charge of many of the public programs and agencies at the local level. The principal issue is whether the black poor will have a role and how they will exercise their influence. Having little institutional control or influence, the only effective lever the poor have is the ballot. The black middle class, on the other hand, has various amounts and types of influence, though nowhere is it absolute (since they rely on funding from the government, foundations, etc.).

To the extent there is conflict, the battle may well be between, on one side, the poor and race politicians who exercise the poor's political clout and, on the other side, the black middle class and others who exercise the institutional power that in practice is more formidable and precise than the blunt instrument represented by black electoral power.

The history of liberal reform is really a history of the triumph of ideas over raw politics. To the extent that blacks rely on raw political power rather than negotiation in the marketplace of ideas, they will be increasingly marginal politically. If, for whatever reason, the black middle class lines up in a coalition to exercise institutional power (as they almost certainly will, at least in part), the stage is set for conflict–both among blacks and with whites, especially neo-liberals who, more than conservatives, will struggle with these issues.

There is also the question of who speaks for blacks–an issue that becomes more urgent as the differences outlined above become clearer. Will it be the race politicians who draw support from the black masses? Or will it be the members of the black business and professional middle class who are aligned with and have a base in multiracial constituencies and institutions?

Of course, there is the possibility of broad coalitions that cut across race and class lines–a scenario, however, that has been successful in only limited spheres, such as in cities where well-organized blacks form a large minority. It has not been successful at the national or state levels, and it is national and state policy that is at the heart of the policy issues I have discussed. Cities have relatively little to do with changing the socioeconomic status of individuals. Part of the present task is to get some perspective on how to help expand the social and economic progress of blacks. To be successful, leadership has to be effective beyond the realm where race politics is effective. There will also have to be new policy ideas; yet the political sphere is not where new ideas typically originate. They most often emerge elsewhere and are tested and refined in the political arena. Black politics and policy in part have to be effective in state and national arenas and in academic and institutional circles where black input is presently sparse.

Taking this course is not simple. It raises two kinds of choices. Do blacks in local elections support race politicians such as Marion Barry or the late Harold Washington, or do they support widely regarded and broadly influential pillars of the black middle class such as the late Patricia Harris or Andrew Young? There is the additional question of whether the black business and professional class (i.e., professors, corporate lawyers, and business leaders) will or will not become active in local politics. What should be the position of "cross over" politicians such as Los Angeles Mayor Tom Bradley? The other kind of choice is between a race politician and a certified friendly white politician who has the ability and interest to take account of black aspirations in national and institutional realms.

The black schism referred to here is in part a matter of two styles: first, the rational analytical style of strategic politics with policy grounded in the professions and business and, second, the "expressive" style of ethnic politics grounded in advocacy of group interests, race solidarity, party loyalty, mass appeal, and alliances of convenience or tradition with liberals. The former is more characteristic of the middle class while the latter reflects the political tradition of the poor. These lines will sharpen within the black community as they have already among white Democrats who, for example, have such camps as "ethnic or urban politician" or "suburban politician"–all under the Democratic umbrella. The interests are real. Each is entitled to a fair and articulate representation around the table. A party cannot claim to a national party if it cannot handle this.

The reader may think that this analysis too sharply draws the divisions within the black community. While the extent of the division cannot be precisely estimated and will vary from place to place and over time, it is a real and it is an important source of tension. The only question is whether the interests of these groups are so mismatched that the tension cannot be made creative or redemptive, thus preventing a much needed dialogue within a black community too long dependent on ideas and initiatives from outside. I don't believe the mismatch will be fatal. I believe that most middle-class blacks want racial progress. I believe that most whites do as well. But I also believe that we are approaching a period where the permanence of the underclass and the frustrations of the rest of society may produce action before dialogue, reaction before analysis.

Whether we have dialogue in the black community is not entirely a policy question or even an institutional one. It is a matter of our personal politics and our capacity to find words to express our concerns and feelings. It is also a matter of trust: whether we can talk openly about our concerns and fears, whether we can trust the resolution of these matters to a political system not noted for its sensitivity to minority concerns and not subject to influence by blacks.

## Conclusion

In this paper I have suggested that blacks lack a clear voice in the major debates over, and the ideological structuring of, those domestic policies that are central in efforts to achieve their aspirations. Because the issues affect blacks differently depending on class and because there have been shifts in the black class structure that have altered traditional ideological positions, the lack of voice is part of, and contributes to, an emerging schism in the black community.

The present paralysis and blindness of collective will in the black community are relatively new. Leaders such as Douglass, Washington, Du Bois and, most recently, King, presented ideas that supported the development of the movement and changed the relationship between the private aspirations of blacks and the political and social action they undertook. King, for example, gave us a voice with which to speak. That voice was powerful in building a coalition, propelling action, and striking with efficient resonance the cords in the national heart. His loss has not been replaced, and the technology of nonviolence has not been transformed to tackle present problems.

While the voice he offered would not have been good for all times, and while evolution was inevitable, we have not as a people evolved. What we have is mounting personal and community anguish and confusion about our relationship to each other and to whites, and about our personal disposition on matters in our community and individual lives. Set adrift as we are, we rely on porous ideological and political floats rather than sturdy vessels that can support navigation with and against the currents in our society.

Among whites, there is also drift. Those committed to racial equality anguish over how to be effective, helpful, and sensitive without being paternalistic, sentimental, or negligent to responsibilities in other areas such as gender or class inequality. They also want to avoid being victims of moral blackmail that plays on guilt. They listen for black voices to lead or share leadership, but hear none. They were conditioned by the black power movement to expect and to respect black self-definition that was partially developed by Carmichael and others but was never carried fully to its institutional, strategic, or personal potential. The movement was like a torch that produced heat and light as long as it burned. When the flame died, there was nothing left. The movement generated expectations among blacks and whites that have not been fulfilled.

For those whites who consider and face the racial issue only out of professional or political necessity, there is also concern. They look at problems blacks face or that society faces and wonder what to do. They sense something different needs to be done but find the language of discourse inadequate. They are alienated by strident voices. They would engage in legitimate dialogue if blacks could only develop a language, identify a forum, and create an environment where fears, suspicions, and concerns could be presented and resolved with dignity and in mutual respect. They know some of the tough questions and hard choices and only the political requirement to build some consensus, a requirement as yet unmet, stays their disposition to "do something." There is no guarantee they will be supportive of black interests. They will have to be convinced that there is an overlap of interests with blacks or that blacks can compel them to pay a cost for inattention.

Then there are whites who are not interested in black advancement, either because they are blind and cannot see its connection to anything of interest to them, or because they have an interest that they feel requires perpetuation of the status quo. They had great freedom to act in the Reagan administration, whose bold assault on blacks gathered momentum largely because it was not effectively challenged. Rather than being skillful social engineers acting on a national mandate against blacks (which public opinion polls suggest does not exist), they are reckless ideologues who have commandeered an economic policy to strike at those fragile structures of justice that are the heart and soul of a democracy.

Black leadership has not met the challenge posed by the changes in ideology and has effectively placed the underclass as well as itself at risk. This need not have happened. Blacks have not had an effective offense. After all, blacks in California did better under Governor Reagan than blacks nationally did under President Reagan. Blacks did better in the South against better led, more organized, and powerful racist forces in the 60s than against less powerful and more diffuse elements in the 80s. That was possible because the moral voice raised by Dr. King was more powerful than the state and private forces mustered against him.

The difference now, I assert, is the lack of a progressive voice, the lack of which has allowed other voices, some hostile to black interests, to fill the vacuum. A new moral and strategic articulation of the just society is called for; and it is important, indeed imperative, that the black community, in all of its manifestations, create the dialogue and debate from which this fresh voice may arise.

# References

Banfield, E.C. (1974). *The Unheavenly City.* Boston: Little, Brown.

Glazer, N. (1975). *Affirmative Discrimination: Ethnic Equality and Public Policy.* New York: Basic Books.

Kristol, I. & Glazer, N. (Eds.). (n.d.). *The Public Interest.* Published quarterly by National Affairs, Inc., Washington, DC.

Murray, C.A. (1984). *Losing Ground.* New York: Basic Books.

Peters, C. (1983, May). The Neo-Liberal Manifesto. *Washington Monthly, 15* (3), 8 18.

Wilson, J.Q. & Heinstein, R.J. (1986). *Crime and Human Nature.* Louisville, KY: Touchstone Books.

# Appendix

## Assessment of the Status of African-Americans Project Study Group Members

### Project Leaders

Director: Wornie L. Reed, William Monroe Trotter Institute, University of Massachusetts at Boston

Co-Chair: James E. Blackwell, Department of Sociology, University of Massachusetts at Boston

Co-Chair: Lucius J. Barker, Department of Political Science, Washington University

### Study Group on Education

Charles V. Willie (Chair), School of Education, Harvard University
Antoine M. Garibaldi (Vice-Chair), Department of Education, Xavier University
Robert A. Dentler, Department of Sociology, University of Massachusetts at Boston
Robert C. Johnson, Minority Studies Academic Program, St. Cloud State University
Meyer Weinberg, Department of Education, University of Massachusetts at Amherst

### Study Group on Employment, Income, and Occupations

William Darity, Jr., (Chair) Department of Economics, University of North Carolina
Barbara Jones (Vice-Chair), College of Business, Prairies View A&M University
Jeremiah P. Cotton, Department of Economics, University of Massachusetts at Boston
Herbert Hill, Industrial Relations Research Institute, University of Wisconsin

### Study Group on Political Participation and the Administration of Justice

Michael B. Preston (Chair), Department of Political Science, University of Southern California
Diane M. Pinderhughes (Vice-Chair), Department of Political Science, University of Illinois/Champaign
Tobe Johnson, Department of Political Science, Morehouse College

Nolan Jones, Staff Director, Committee on Criminal Justice and Public Protection, National Governors Association
Susan Welch, Department of Political Science, University of Nebraska
John Zipp, Department of Sociology, University of Wisconsin-Milwaukee

## Study Group on Social and Cultural Change

Alphonso Pinkney (Chair), Department of Sociology, Hunter College
James Turner (Vice-Chair), Africana Studies and Research Center, Cornell University
John Henrik Clarke, Department of Black and Puerto Rican Studies, Hunter College
Sidney Wilhelm, Department of Sociology, State University of New York-Buffalo

## Study Group on Health Status and Medical Care

William Darity, Sr. (Chair), School of Public Health, University of Massachusetts at Amherst
Stanford Roman (Vice-Chair), Morehouse School of Medicine, Atlanta
Claudia Baquet, National Cancer Institute, Bethesda, Maryland
Noma L. Roberson, Department of Cancer Control and Epidemiology, Rockwell Park Institute

## Study Group on the Family

Robert B. Hill (Chair), Morgan State University, Baltimore, Maryland
Andrew Billingsley (Vice-Chair), Department of Family and Community Development, University of Maryland
Eleanor Engram, Engram-Miller Associates, Cleveland, Ohio
Michelene R. Malson, School of Social Work, University of North Carolina
Roger H. Rubin, Department of Family and Community Development, University of Maryland
Carol B. Stack, Graduate School of Education, University of California-Berkeley
James B. Stewart, Black Studies Program, Pennsylvania State University
James E. Teele, Department of Sociology, Boston University

# Contributors

Carolyne W. Arnold, College of Public and Community Services, University of Massachusetts at Boston
James Banks, School of Education, University of Washington
Margaret Beale Spencer, College of Education, Emory University
Bob Blauner, Department of Sociology, University of California, Berkeley
Larry Carter, Department of Sociology, University of Oregon
Obie Clayton, School of Criminal Justice, University of Nebraska
James P. Comer, Department of Psychiatry, Yale Medical School
Charles Flowers, Department of Education, Fisk University
Bennett Harrison, Urban and Public Affairs, Carnegie Mellon University
Norris M. Haynes, Child Study Center, New Haven
Joseph Himes, Department of Sociology, University of North Carolina at Greensboro
Hubert E. Jones, School of Social Work, Boston University
James M. Jones, Department of Psychology, University of Delaware
Faustine C. Jones-Wilson, *Journal of Negro Education*, Howard University
Barry A. Kreisberg, National Council on Crime and Delinquency, San Francisco
Hubert G. Locke, Society of Justice Program, University of Washington
E. Yvonne Moss, William Monroe Trotter Institute, University of Massachusetts at Boston
Willie Pearson, Jr., Department of Sociology, Grambling State University
Michael L. Radelet, Department of Sociology, University of Florida
Robert Rothman, *Education Week*, Washington, DC
Diana T. Slaughter, School of Education, Northwestern University
A. Wade Smith, Department of Sociology, Arizona State University
Leonard Stevens, Compact for Educational Opportunity, Milwaukee
Wilbur Watson, Department of Sociology, Atlanta University
Warren Whatley, Department of Economics, University of Michigan
John B. Williams, Affirmative Action Office, Harvard University
Rhonda Williams, Department of Economics, University of Maryland
Reginald Wilson, American Council of Education, Washington, DC